First World War
and Army of Occupation
War Diary
France, Belgium and Germany

15 DIVISION
Divisional Troops
32 Sanitary Section
1 August 1915 - 28 February 1917

WO95/1932/2

The Naval & Military Press Ltd
www.nmarchive.com
Published in association with The National Archives

Published by

The Naval & Military Press Ltd

Unit 10 Ridgewood Industrial Park,

Uckfield, East Sussex,

TN22 5QE England

Tel: +44 (0) 1825 749494

www.naval-military-press.com

www.nmarchive.com

This diary has been reprinted in facsimile from the original. Any imperfections are inevitably reproduced and the quality may fall short of modern type and cartographic standards.

© **Crown Copyright**
Images reproduced by permission of The National Archives, London, England, 2015.

Contents

Document type	Place/Title	Date From	Date To
Heading	WO95/1932/2		
Heading	15th Division 32nd Sanitary Section Aug 1915-1917 Feb To 3rd Army		
Heading	15th Division Summarised But Not Copied 32nd Sanitary Section Vol I August 15-Dec 1916		
Heading	Confidential Diary S.H. Daukes Lt. RAMC (L) Sanitary Sector 32 Attached To XV Division August 1915		
War Diary	Cosnay	01/08/1915	03/08/1915
War Diary	Hesdigneuil	04/08/1915	31/08/1915
Miscellaneous	Previous Sanitary Continuances Used In XV Division Aug 1915		
Heading	15th Division Summarised But Not Copied 32nd Sanitary Section Vol. II Sept. 15		
Miscellaneous	No. 32 San Sect Sept. 1915		
Heading	Confidential Diary For Sept. 1915 Capt Res. D.A.L.C. (T) O.C. 32 Sanitary Sector Attached To 15 Div		
War Diary	Hesdigneul	01/09/1915	23/09/1915
War Diary	Hesdigneuil & Noeux Les Mines.	24/09/1915	24/09/1915
War Diary	Noeux Les Mines	25/09/1915	28/09/1915
War Diary	Hesdigneuil	29/09/1915	29/09/1915
War Diary	La Buissiere	30/09/1915	30/09/1915
Heading	15th Division Summarised But Not Copied 32nd Sanitary Section Vol. I Oct 15		
Heading	Confidential War Diary Of Capt. S.H. Daukes O.C San Sec 32 Att XV Div. B.E.F.		
War Diary	La Buissiere	01/10/1915	02/10/1915
War Diary	Lapugnoy	03/10/1915	18/10/1915
War Diary	Noeux Les Mines	19/10/1915	31/10/1915
Heading	Summarised But Not Copied No. 32 Sanitary Section. October 1915		
Heading	Confidential Diary 32nd Sanitary Sector Att 15th Division October 1915		
War Diary	La Buissiere	01/10/1915	02/10/1915
War Diary	Lapugnoy	03/10/1915	16/10/1915
War Diary	Noeux-Les Mines	17/10/1915	31/10/1915
Heading	15th Division Summarised But Not Copied 32 San. Section Nov 15		
Heading	Confidential War Diary Sanitary Section 32 November 1915		
War Diary	Noeux Les Mines	01/11/1915	26/11/1915
War Diary	Drouvin	27/11/1915	30/11/1915
Miscellaneous	Appendix I		
Heading	15th Division F/254/1 Summarised But Not Copied December 1915		
Heading	Confidential Diary Dec 1915 Sanitary Sec 32 Of 2nd Land Sanitary Co C. Div. XV B.E.F.		
War Diary	Drouvin	01/12/1915	14/12/1915
War Diary	Lillers	15/12/1915	31/12/1915
War Diary		18/12/1915	18/12/1915
Heading	15th Division F/254/2 32 San. Section Jan 1916		

Heading	Sanitary Sec 32 2nd London Sanitary Co. Confidential War Diary January 1916		
War Diary	Lillers	01/01/1916	05/01/1916
Miscellaneous	Appendix I		
War Diary	Lillers Erny St. Julien	05/01/1916	05/01/1916
War Diary	Erny St Julien	06/01/1916	06/01/1916
War Diary	Lillers	07/01/1916	14/01/1916
War Diary	Noeux Les Mines	15/01/1916	31/01/1916
Heading	15th Div. 32nd Sany Section Feb 1916		
Miscellaneous	32 Sanitary Section Vol VII		
Heading	Confidential War Diary Sanitary Section. 32 att 15th Div February 1916		
War Diary	Noeux Les Mines	01/02/1916	09/02/1916
War Diary	Noeux	10/02/1916	12/02/1916
War Diary	Noeux Les Mines	13/02/1916	29/02/1916
Heading	War Diaries of 32nd Sanitary Section-15th Division For the month of March and April 1916		
Heading	Confidential Diary Sanitary Section 32 attached 15th Div. B.E.F. March. 1916		
War Diary	Noeux-Les-Mines	01/03/1916	27/03/1916
War Diary	Lillers	28/03/1916	31/03/1916
Heading	Sanitary Section 32 Attached 15th Div April 1916. Confidential Diary		
War Diary	Lillers	01/04/1916	26/04/1916
War Diary	Sailly	27/04/1916	30/04/1916
Heading	Confidential War Diary San Sec 32 Attd 15th Division May. 1916. Vol 10		
War Diary	Sailly	01/05/1916	12/05/1916
War Diary	Sailly. La Bourse	13/05/1916	17/05/1916
War Diary	Sailly	18/05/1916	31/05/1916
War Diary	Sailly La Bourse	31/05/1916	31/05/1916
Miscellaneous	Appendix B Define Collection Scheme.		
Miscellaneous	Appendix C. Preliminary Report On Experiments Carried Out With "C" Solution		
Miscellaneous	Appendix D		
Miscellaneous	Appendix E Trench Sanitation (Summary of report by Inspector L/C Townend)		
Heading	32 San Sec Vol II June 1916		
Heading	Confidential War Diary San Sec 32 Attd 15th Div June 1916		
War Diary	Sailly	01/06/1916	30/06/1916
Heading	Confidential War Diary San Sec 32 Attd 15th Div July 1916. Vol. 12		
War Diary	Sailly La Bourse	01/07/1916	06/07/1916
War Diary	Sailly	07/07/1916	21/07/1916
War Diary	Bryas	22/07/1916	25/07/1916
War Diary	Flers	26/07/1916	26/07/1916
War Diary	Frohen-Le-Grand	27/07/1916	27/07/1916
War Diary	Bernaville	28/07/1916	30/07/1916
War Diary	Vignacourt	31/07/1916	31/07/1916
Heading	15th Div. Confidential War Diary August 1916 Sanitary Section 32 Of 2nd Lond Sanitary C. Attd 15th Div.		
War Diary	Vignacourt	01/08/1916	03/08/1916
War Diary	St Gratien	04/08/1916	04/08/1916
War Diary	Baizieux	05/08/1916	07/08/1916
War Diary	Albert	08/08/1916	12/08/1916

War Diary	N.W. Albert	13/08/1916	15/08/1916
War Diary	Albert	16/08/1916	22/08/1916
War Diary	W Of. Albert	23/08/1916	24/08/1916
War Diary	W Of Albert E8.a.8.2	25/08/1916	29/08/1916
War Diary	E8a8.2	29/08/1916	31/08/1916
Miscellaneous	Unit Inspection Appendix 1		
Heading	War Diary 32 Sanitary Sec. 15th Div. September 1916		
War Diary	E 8a82 E7C4.3 Albert Can Sheet	01/09/1916	04/09/1916
War Diary	Combined Albert Sheet E7C43	05/09/1916	12/09/1916
War Diary	E7C43	13/09/1916	30/09/1916
Heading	15th Div 32nd Sanitary Section Oct. 1916		
Heading	Confidential Diary Sanitary Section 32 Attd 15 Div October 1916		
War Diary	Albert Area E7C43	01/10/1916	02/10/1916
War Diary	Montigny III Corps "B" Sanitary Area	03/10/1916	31/10/1916
Heading	War Diary 32 Sanitary Section 15th Div November 1916 Vol 16		
War Diary	Montigny III Corps "B" Sanitary Area.	01/11/1916	30/11/1916
Heading	War Diary Month of December 1916 Capt A E-Jury RAMC (T) O.C. 32 Sanitary Section L. Forward Area III Corps IV Army		
War Diary	Field	01/12/1916	31/12/1916
Heading	15th Div. 32nd Sanitary Section. Jan 1917		
Heading	Diary Sanitary Section 32 att XV Div January 1917 Vol 18		
War Diary		01/01/1917	31/01/1917
Heading	15th Div. 32nd Sanitary Section. Feb. 1917		
Heading	Diary Sanitary Section 32 att XV Divn February 1917. Vol 19		
War Diary		01/02/1917	28/02/1917

MO95/19342

15TH DIVISION

32ND SANITARY SECTION
AUG 1915 - DEC 1916
1917 FEB

To 3rd ARMY

121/6753

15ᵗʰ Kiroku

Summarised but not copied

32ⁿᵈ Sanitary Section

vol II

August 15
–
Dec 1916

August 16

Army Form C. 2118.

WAR DIARY
or
INTELLIGENCE SUMMARY

(Erase heading not required.)

Hour, Date, Place	Summary of Events and Information	Remarks and references to Appendices
	CONFIDENTIAL DIARY J.H. DAUKES Lt RAMC(S) Sanitary Section 32 Attached to XI Division	August 1915

Instructions regarding War Diaries and Intelligence Summaries are contained in F. S. Regs., Part II. and the Staff Manual respectively. Title pages will be prepared in manuscript.

Army Form C. 2118.

WAR DIARY
or
INTELLIGENCE SUMMARY.
(Erase heading not required.)

Instructions regarding War Diaries and Intelligence Summaries are contained in F. S. Regs., Part II. and the Staff Manual respectively. Title pages will be prepared in manuscript.

Place	Date	Hour	Summary of Events and Information	Remarks and references to Appendices
GOSNAY	1.8.15		Inspected new headquarters for Sr Div at Y'DROUIN. Cleansing very necessary. Staying with French colonel. Suggestions made re latrine accommodation, supply etc — All suggestions to be carried out tomorrow. Drainage work undertaken by fatigue party at background. To get rid of pools of pale stagnant water in cemetery.	JPH
	2.8.15		Squads 1, 2, 3 working at DROUIN, cleansing carried out by fatigue party in all direction of water supply section. Double tent carried on by squad 2.	JPH
	3.8.15		4pm at DROUIN — work completed as far as possible. Details still needing attention (1) Cm pit outside latrine well interrupted drain (2) water supply not very satisfactory owing to defective pump. Visited BETHUNE with ADMS re scheme for putting troops in charge from N.E. is most likely evolution of new billets. Squad 2 detailed to deal with this matter. Arranged for squad 3 & 5 from opened and at NOEUX LES MINES from Thursday 5 inst.	JPH

Army Form C. 2118.

WAR DIARY
or
INTELLIGENCE SUMMARY
(Erase heading not required.)

Place	Date	Hour	Summary of Events and Information	Remarks and references to Appendices
HESDIGNEUIL 4	4.8.15		Distribution of grads from today (1) RAUDRICOURT (2) NOEUX LES MINES (3) NOEUX LES MINES (4) HESDIGNEUIL. Forms drafted for daily & weekly returns. Kit at Ch. DROUVIN enfluent Pond sanitation now in satisfactory condition. Other squad continue work. Shed sanitary work carried out at Drouvin — connection with water supply, field kitchens & latrines.	[sig]
5	4.8.15		Squad work at 1st Div: 3 is flyproofing mens kitchens etc. Laundry area being cleaned & fatigue party under supervision. Dental Relief Station at (1) NOEUX LES MINES, MAZINGARBE.	
	6.7.15		LE RIERIS. Squad disinfecting work at MAZINGARBE hospital. S/S Visited NOEUX-LES-MINES hospital — disinfection etc re scarlet fever case carried out. Infected billets instructions re geese traps to hospital. Infected billets in the BREBIS hospital. 6 cases of infected poultry condition in MEROC & the trenches. Nos 7 squad 1 + 11 of 794 at Drouvin. Routine work elsewhere.	[sig]

WAR DIARY
INTELLIGENCE SUMMARY

Army Form C. 2118.

Place	Date	Hour	Summary of Events and Information	Remarks and references to Appendices
HERDIGNEUL	7/8/45		D.I attended demonstration by gas expert. Demonstrated model latrine area to representatives of I.C. 45-46. The experiment to find a creosote/cresol mixture of 100 known tried on a new extended scale. Good work carried on at NAUDRICOURT, HOUCHIN, DROUIN, NOEUX LES MINES. Disinfecting lorries arrived, one sent over to I.A. 47.	See G/Dis 1. 87/0
"	8/8/45		Demonstrated model latrine area to representatives of I.A. 47. Threat disinfector brought over I. two lorries from Army outward for road transport. Hired native workmen over CE new area. Laundry are being prepared. Mobile latrines being enlarged to accommodate 50 men. That over 15 St. Cometh C2l are well set-up. ABC's also navigated contain. Drawn in of ASC informed. Suggested in lorry area. The district for commandants purpose is now divided up	87/0
"	9/8/45			

WAR DIARY
INTELLIGENCE SUMMARY.
(Erase heading not required.)

Army Form C. 2118.

Instructions regarding War Diaries and Intelligence Summaries are contained in F.S. Regs., Part II. and the Staff Manual respectively. Title pages will be prepared in manuscript.

Place	Date	Hour	Summary of Events and Information	Remarks and references to Appendices
HESDIGNEUIL	10.8.15		as follows. Sqd I. Cross all work between Noyelles & HOUCHIN. Sqd II. All work & Roads from NOEUX LES MINES to the trenches. Sqd III. the HOUCHIN, NOEUX LES MINES area. All sqds instructed as follows – memoranda must be kept where tactical considerations permit; no refuse pits will be allowed in the divisional area of such where tactical cannot be held, in such case of such other how must immediately be cleaned & disinfected. All tins, bits & sledges pits to be covered in & then 6 miles of filter bed rowed. Met an tincks in front of QUALITY STREET & PHILOSOPHE area. Pantoton similar to Metrod one dept for burial of sqd III. S. sqd and hand and ten ales. Temporard (?) and sqd to flags at night.	SH75
"	11.8.15		Sqd III. Fung disinfectin at NOEUX LES MINES hospital II. Hyghly cleaning billets GOE vented model Latrine idea. Proceed week to build in HESDIGNEUIL, RAUDRICOURT, DROUVIN. One & dummy quart for 4 officers of N. S. A.	SH75 SH75

WAR DIARY or INTELLIGENCE SUMMARY

Army Form C. 2118.

Place	Date	Hour	Summary of Events and Information	Remarks and references to Appendices
HESDIGNEUIL	12/8/15		Inspected Signal Coys at DIEUVAL; much attention needed. T3/O much h.gr. Arranged for officer latrine & decligraphers. Arrangts made with Staff Seg're create Laundry for 1st Div. Centres work throughout division. The mineral ophalt (made into lime etc) in that they cannot expire to Sanitary standard owing to lack of men & necessary fatigue duties.	
"	13/8/15		Clearing of ground left from 9 47 ? in hedgerows. Action taken in nature to affect, from over of holt. Report for A.S. of M, but latrine system is not necessary. Visited NOEUX LES MINES. MARINGATRE LESTREM is all B.A.D.m.S. Investigated enteric trouble Artillery line (office not satisfactory) college corps. Veeds to N.e M with the Burial Increased scheme of work arranged to Informers of Artillery line.	
"	14/8/15		Visited HOUCHIN — no wtr — mounds, left with ADMS. NOEUVILLE MINES in latrine & intals. Doctors but carried out by squads.	

1577 Wt.W10791/1773 500,000 1/15 D.D.&.L A.D.S.S./Forms/C. 2118.

Place	Date	Hour	Summary of Events and Information	Remarks and references to Appendices
HESDIG NEUX	15/8/15		Note work. Such rating as far as possible. Interviewed squad NCOs. Generated round parts incog. Certain to speed Pm. RGA visited NOEUX L. MINES, MAZINGARBE with DADMS. Inspected Billets 1 Gunnr 1 S. Garths, dealt with sundry points raised by S/Sgt Bleed re h.qu 47 F.a. All billets in eight fm Watersaching + thorough cleansing arg. made through AA QMG for regular White-washing of huts. He lights here to be removed. Checking of Bolts noted at LE BREBIS fm turfy & Serg. e Blanch.	
"	17/8/15		Visited with ADMS NOEUX-LES-MINES, LE BREBIS. Saw bathing arrangements at mines. Interviewed MO & CO 10 L.N. at am billet. Ordered a sanitorn. just difficult in this respect with area occupied by up 48 hrs at most, enter absolutely latrine system choked with ? daily with ??? Interviewed squad 2 VL in a ork hrg due h?d?d down to Watersby billets. Saw trench latrine at L BREBIS recently	q 47 F.a.

WAR DIARY
or
INTELLIGENCE SUMMARY.
(Erase heading not required).

Army Form C 2118.

Place.	Date	Hour	Summary of Events and Information.	Remarks and references to Appendices
HESDIGNEUIL	18/8/15		Visited MAZINGARBE at request of ADMS to investigate bathing facilities situated in PHILOSOPHE, constantly under shell fire; no bathing facilities. Also visited Zone 3 at NOEUX LES MINES; neg. result but hear that there are facilities at Zone 4 (Stones). Visited billets & horses in MAZINGARBE. Much doing. Visited D.A.D. and at LE BREBIS. The condition of sanitary problems in area occupied for very short period (48 hrs) & areas where after 12 days the water is not available. Infected billets etc. Visited rats used for bathing purposes; mangers cleaned out used, etc to be erected.	
"	19/8/15		Visited corps of A.S.C. Div. Am. Col. 7, Am. Col. 72, Corps Int. had great improvement in cap sanitation. Visited 4 S.F.C. & A.D.M.S. regards certain clothing to be carried at each spinner of sanitary Sqn.	
"	20/8/15		Visited 71st F.A. Subs machine gun section. Cavalry & Div Goldtr. (with SADMS) Improvement since last visit at still much to be done. Remained are frequently not emptied, by too low to be effective work. Final toilette is excellent except in last naval unit. The one taken too seriously. The defects H.L. Unit is now known instead of being (wastly) & G.S.L. Infected area occupied by sanitary squad & sergeant selfsection with commd sanitary entrance.	

WAR DIARY or INTELLIGENCE SUMMARY

Army Form C 2118.

Place	Date	Hour	Summary of Events and Information.	Remarks and references to Appendices
HERDIGNEUIL	21/8/15		Special visits to 45 F.A. 73 R.F.A. Signal Co. 7 R.F.A. A.C. great improvement in sanitary condition. Squads engaged in routine work. Probably check urine & rectage fields for refuse pits are being adopted in most units: incinerators being managed daily. not the theoretical model are intended for. Fly reduction to a minimum.	JHS
"	22/8/15		Visit to hospital & Refts at NOEUX LES MINES with A.D.M.S. Much improvement since my last visit to the latter. Squads 2 & 3 are now meeting every Refts daily	JHS
"	23/8/15		Interviewed Squad NCO's. Talked over various schemes. Volume not arrived for use during week: four needed up & needed attention at HERDIGNEUIL. Spent office of ADMS. Visited 8 artillery corps with Major Wood: advised upon various sanitary matters. Fixed to have some effected where for building, incineration of standard & useful pattern.	JHS
"	24/8/15		Complete inspection of MARINGARBE Refts etc. If possible the area should be treated as a permanent camp for sanitary accommodation & shut trades be adopted, a few definite areas being set aside for incineration, incinerators put & latrines Volume not up to date & could not be used.	JHS

Stationery Services Press, X 8, 5,000 7/15

WAR DIARY
or
INTELLIGENCE SUMMARY
(Erase heading not required).

Army Form C 2118.

Place.	Date	Hour	Summary of Events and Information.	Remarks and references to Appendices
HESDIGNEUIL	25/8/15		Visited VAUDRICOURT & NEUX LES MINES. Inspected camps & arranged work. Sergt. Beach reported sick & admitted to hospital 47th F.A. Brigade 2 + 3 charged effort to left above Bath house.	JHD
	27/8/15		Routine work and progress. S/Sgt. Beach still in rest station. Visited 46 F.A. & other R.E. units with A.D.M.S. Visited in case at MALINGATRE at 112 H.B.	JHD
	28/8/15		Visited NOEUX LES MINES with A.D.M.S. Arranged about various details regarding units to be carried in in view of extension of area, two new groups LE BRERIS but includes GONAY, FOUQUIERES & LA TOURIERE. Staff Sergt. reta. in hospital.	JHD
	29/8/15		Routine work carried on. Heavy rain interfered with incineration of excreta. It is practically impossible to have a supply of coal in the face of the ASC found any great improvement in the means as to succeed in bad weather.	JHD
	30/8/15		Visited MARINGARRE re questions of permanent sanitary areas. Visited ASC Camps with A.D.M.S. who seemed general sanitary arrangements of Squad working on routine lines.	JHD

Army Form C. 2118.

WAR DIARY
or
INTELLIGENCE SUMMARY

(Erase heading not required.)

Hour, Date, Place	Summary of Events and Information	Remarks and references to Appendices
31/8/15. HESDIGNEUL	Until NOEUX LES MINES reinforcements in fantry Area routine; areas sufficient. Inspected scheme for manoeuvre of units at VERQUIN. Emerged for exercise at Headquarters at DIEVAL R.T.A. to be used at Headquarters of QMG & 72 Battery R.T.A. Interviewed AA & QMG re 72 Battery R.T.A. Summary This month has seen much improvement in general routine arrangements in the division. A uniform scheme is gradually being adopted in units; manoeuvre of a good pattern. Horses with sledge for feed & crowd Horse pits yelmed type etc etc Incinerators, grease traps in cond. at Hrs. Canteen Latrines etc to take in wet weather. There has been recent letter infection amongst horses in the general orders not has been very low.	[signature]

Various sanitary contrivances used in
XI Division   Aug. 1915
Burnt tin Latrines. The contents are burnt
in a beehive incinerator immediately after deposit.

(A) Two tins. upper perforated
    lower not perforated.
    Motions falls onto straw
    urine passes into cresol pit.
    upper tin cut & splayed
    out so as to form
    front & back guards.
    Tin slides out on ledge
    A B
    The lower tin is
    emptied when necessary

cresol 5%

(A) [diagram labelled: handle, handle, straw, B, A, cresol 5%]

(B) [diagram: 2, tin, tin, Brick & tin drain, X, Y, urine funnel]

(B) upper tins as
in A, but urine passes into
drain XY which can be flushed
through trap Z. Urine passing
straight into urine pit
made of ordinary model type.
An ordinary rough wooden seat is used
with these Latrines.

Urine pits and pits for sullage water are closed after being filled in with tins (bottoms knocked out) bricks (broken) & stones in the usual manner.
Grease traps are made of the following varieties

- upper tin as shewn to catch vegetables etc from Dixies
- hay etc
- Tin drain
- Soakage pit
- clinker or sands

In some cases the upper tin is not used but is certainly an improvement.
Urine is led into urine pits through funnels, perforated tins, impervious channels or troughs

- pit
- drain
- The trough which is triangular in section is made by cutting a biscuit tin diagonally

12/6971

15th Division

Summarised but not copied

32nd Sanitary Section.
Vol: II

Sept. 15

Sept 15

15

No. 32 San. Sect.
Sept. '915
___

App. A. has been detached & filed under "Sanitation Water"

___

CONFIDENTIAL DIARY
of Sept. 1915.

of Capt Saunders. R.A.M.C (T)
O.C. 3rd Sanitary Sect
attached to 15 Div.

WAR DIARY
or
INTELLIGENCE SUMMARY

Hour, Date, Place	Summary of Events and Information	Remarks and references to Appendices
1/9/15 HERDIGNEUL	Noted to BEUVRIERE inflicted 68 los. transport of 7 KOSB & 12 HLI many sanitary improvements needed throughout. MO & In dodid line of permanent camp P. sta lodge & pl OCurrie to superintend the work. Met road congh & superintd the extra also infected ground site for 45 F.A. also infected ground site for small Bath House. Supply on sit of C.o. DROUIN ready by to each of pump leaking. Craig's made 2 x day squad carrying in more water.	Attack
2/9/15 "	Visited DROUIN & VAUDRICOURT. The area is now crowded & blocked by the arrival of units from Div 1, & Div 4,7. Squads 1 & 4 now at HERDIGNEUL.	Attack Hawley (Cafe to be closed)
3/9/15	Heavy rain all day. Deaths infection carried at. Cess pit at Brown infected. Considerable movements of troops expected onwards.	Attack Jawkes

WAR DIARY
or
INTELLIGENCE SUMMARY

(Erase heading not required.)

Army Form C. 2118.

Hour, Date, Place	Summary of Events and Information	Remarks and references to Appendices
4/9/15 HESDIGNEUIL	Invited new bodyguard. Scheme of sanitation arranged.	JHW
6/9/15	Route not covered. Investigation of water supplies at PHILOSOPHE, QUALITIES REMELLES. Excellent supply & plenty at the last named place. Thus wells of forts = 7.9 m. 3 will towers & mill & whole June a-abundant & excellent supply. Good wooded farm in BEUVRIERE as to thoroughfare now moved in. Visited MO at NEDRICOURT. info of 40 H.B. of othrs had detailed certain men of S.S. & corry m but many from field canties to lay men very Anglyn of our vent in engineers too greatly at say 12 footsteps stead. Nee 1 case to watch for in taking.	
7/9/15	"	JHW
8/9/15	Sanitary inspection of REBQUIN recently recvd by 1st Div. the two close used as infirmary & out Dev. left by J.S. not for purvele Dev	

WAR DIARY
or
INTELLIGENCE SUMMARY

(Erase heading not required.)

Army Form C. 2118.

Hour, Date, Place	Summary of Events and Information	Remarks and references to Appendices
8/9/15 HESDIGNEUIL	[handwritten entry, largely illegible] ... VAUDRICOURT ... PERNOIS ...	
9/9/15	[handwritten entry]	

Army Form C. 2118.

WAR DIARY
or
INTELLIGENCE SUMMARY
(Erase heading not required.)

Instructions regarding War Diaries and Intelligence Summaries are contained in F. S. Regs., Part II. and the Staff Manual respectively. Title pages will be prepared in manuscript.

Hour, Date, Place	Summary of Events and Information	Remarks and references to Appendices
9/9/15 HERDIGNEUIL	attended to Inspection proceeding at NOEUX LES MINES & MAZINGARBE but difficult to obtain transport & fatigue men owing to military situation.	JHB
10/9/15	Special meeting all works - LA BOURTIERE, VERQUIN - General work - NOEUX LES MINES MAZINGARBE.	JHB
11/9/15	Work at VERQUIN completed and sent forward. Permd went to La BOURTIERE returning. 3 regimental medical officers visited billets. Cafés. Nothing to report.	JHB
12/9/15	Routine work of inspection & making defects good. Permd went to MAZINGARBE, NOEUX LES MINES & VERQUIN returning.	JHB
13/9/15	No. of 7 Canons. The pumping arrangements at VERQUIN often very difficult at times of catastrophes to the pump	JHB

1247 W 32250 200,000 (E) 8/14 J.B.C. & A. Forms C. 2118/11.

Army Form C. 2118.

WAR DIARY
or
INTELLIGENCE SUMMARY
(Erase heading not required.)

Hour, Date, Place	Summary of Events and Information	Remarks and references to Appendices
HESDIGNEUIL 14/9/15	Demonstration to 50 water duty men as to method of water for tanks in the trenches & starting stations. Field Lt. MAZINGARBE during station.	See summary
	Squads carrying in water & working kit to NOEUX LES MINES re work of incidence set.	JH
15/9/15	Demonstration to 15 water duty men at Hotel RETHUNE to Lieut. Visited HESDIGNEUIL. Party studying water in the trenches. Application for studying ob. VERMELLES & S'. M... Squad carrying in water inspections. Got fresh supply of water and clothed went to field cooker.	
16/9/15	Paid section of a section indicated. Arranged work for next week conditions for next week. Routine work as usual.	
17/9/15	Routine inspections carried out.	JH
18/9/15	Visited MAZINGARBE etc re return for studying sources of water in trenches. Interviewed every units of section re work to be done during attack advance.	JH

1247 W 3299 200,000 (E) 8/14 J.B.C.&A. Forms/C.2118/11.

Army Form C. 2118.

WAR DIARY
or
INTELLIGENCE SUMMARY
(Erase heading not required.)

Instructions regarding War Diaries and Intelligence Summaries are contained in F. S. Regs, Part II. and the Staff Manual respectively. Title pages will be prepared in manuscript.

Hour, Date, Place	Summary of Events and Information	Remarks and references to Appendices
19/9/15 HESDIGNEUL	Much noting. Sanitary work in abeyance owing to military situation. Scheme affected to alling action. Probable unit, except to the regiment, to carry out ordinary sanitary duties.	Appx
20/9/15	Studying situation. Taking up of trench took place. Plans taken are not yet settled. The trenches extreme in heavy weather for the moment went during time at the front. Free from the advance dress, also for walk. Column of troops on the march.	Appx
21/9/15	Demonstration to NCOs (eng.) a lecture for the metallic former. Inf. Regd. & C.° howled x Historical cyclists engaged with regard to their in trenches from 7 headquarter for work. Battle tactics during the attack.	Appx Appx

22/9/15
23/9/15

WAR DIARY or INTELLIGENCE SUMMARY

Army Form C. 2118.

Hour, Date, Place	Summary of Events and Information	Remarks and references to Appendices
24/9/15 HESDIGNEUL & NOEUX LES MINES	The new ambulance station detailed for ambulance work as follows — 9 to 47 Field Ambulance NOEUX LES MINES, 11 to Advanced dressing Station PHILOSOPHE. 5 remain at HESDIGNEUIL at coll[ecting] place 2 cars kept in reserve for necessary evacuation duties, infantry ambulance work if required. 1 Officer signaled in charge of LP[?] Marcelle & [illegible] motor cars. C.O. of schme[?] untang arrgt unloadg tinkd[?] with their own in 47 Field Ambulance, rest of sect	JHs
25/9/15 NOEUX LES MINES	Convoy — duties with their own ambulances Lorry convoy wounded between PHILOSOPHE & 46 F.A. Five of the section performed useful work in the operating theatre of 47 F.A.	JHs

WAR DIARY or INTELLIGENCE SUMMARY

Army Form C. 2118.

(Erase heading not required.)

Hour, Date, Place	Summary of Events and Information	Remarks and references to Appendices
26/9/15 NOEUX LES MINES	All members of section busy at ambulance & first aid work. Some during the needed offerms, some looking after Church work, toilet etc. Some as stretcher bearers, some in conducting & feeding the wounded, some carrying wounded from supplies, rations etc.	JHS
27/9/15 "	Ambulances very busy. Took in 26 bt	JHS
28/9/15 "	Ambulances returned to HESDIGNEUIL	JHS
29/9/15 HESDIGNEUIL	XII Division now billeted round HOUDAIN area inspected by various members of Sanitary Section, work made to arrange area of work. Reports received on all billeting areas.	JHS
30/9/15 LA BOUSSIERE	Section moved from HESDIGNEUIL to LA BUISSIÈRE by lorry took 3 journeys	JHS

Army Form C. 2118.

WAR DIARY
or
INTELLIGENCE SUMMARY
(Erase heading not required.)

Instructions regarding War Diaries and Intelligence Summaries are contained in F. S. Regs., Part II. and the Staff Manual respectively. Title pages will be prepared in manuscript.

Hour, Date, Place	Summary of Events and Information	Remarks and references to Appendices
Summary for Sept	The section has carried out routine work of inspection & instruction with satisfactory results. Military practice inspired full sanitary work. We not prevent but gave an opportunity to the section to lower in advance with Reports speak highly of the work carried out during the battle of Loos. Large tanks were installed in the trenches these were carefully inspected by the section and all water supplies of accurate chlorination. Sect was in charge of a new man who was instructed in the duties of me. A. Hawkins, Cpl. O.C. S- Sec 32	See Appendices to Sept. Diary (7)

121/7431

15th
25/10/ Ataraein

Summerroud but not copied

32nd Sanitary Section
Vol: I

Oct 15

15/
Oct 1915

Confidential war diary
of CAPT. S. H. DAUKES
O.C. San Sec. 32
alt XV Div.   B.E.F

Army Form C. 2118.

WAR DIARY
or
INTELLIGENCE SUMMARY
(Erase heading not required.)

Hour, Date, Place	Summary of Events and Information	Remarks and references to Appendices
1/10/15 LA BUISSIERE	Section carrying out conducting manœuvre etc	
2/10/15	General inspection of area occupied by 1st Div. HOUCHIN, HALLICOURT, LA BOURSIERE. Sanitary arrangements, field report in billets, water supplies, cesspits etc	
3/10/15 LAPUGNOY	Orders to move to LA BOURRIETTE district. Completed by 7 p.m. new quarters LAPUGNOY	
4/10/15 "	Sect. carrying out examining water supply. Putting up incinerators, officers meals etc	
5/10/15 "	Camp in order. Free report in water supply directions given with regard to control etc. Double carts commenced.	
6/10/15	Section carrying out routine inspections between LAPUGNOY and LILLERS.	

Army Form C. 2118.

WAR DIARY
or
INTELLIGENCE SUMMARY

(Erase heading not required.)

Instructions regarding War Diaries and Intelligence Summaries are contained in F. S. Regs., Part II. and the Staff Manual respectively. Title pages will be prepared in manuscript.

Hour, Date, Place	Summary of Events and Information	Remarks and references to Appendices
7/10/15 - LAPUGNOY	Arrangements made for work during period of stay in district. Squads 2 & 3 to form 47. F.A. at LILLERS. Nos 9 & 10 at ghost.	FFS
8/10/15	General routine work carried out by section. All units to be inspected & all section to be satisfactory type.	FFS
	Sanitary arrangement Sat Oct 16: of sickness in the division continues to show very low percentage	FFS
9/10/15	Routine work. Latrine check to report	FFS
10/10/15	Squads working	FFS
11/10/15	Routine work, inspection etc all defects being remedied	FFS
12/10/15	Routine work	FFS
13/10/15	Routine work	FFS

Army Form C. 2118.

WAR DIARY
or
INTELLIGENCE SUMMARY
(Erase heading not required.)

Instructions regarding War Diaries and Intelligence Summaries are contained in F. S. Regs., Part II. and the Staff Manual respectively. Title pages will be prepared in manuscript.

Hour, Date, Place	Summary of Events and Information	Remarks and references to Appendices
14/10/15	Routine work	
	Units going trouble free to machine gun section	
	72 D & F A & B Battery 70° Ammunition col	
	All defect material subsequently	
15/10/15	Squads 2 & 3 reported section	
	under orders to move to move	
	Lieut Young C Dow - officer noticed	
	O.C returned from leave	
16/10/15	Section moved (2 lochs) to NOEUX LES MINES	
	New camp stoves in BETHUNE Na	
	Communication allowances sent to Duke	
	of York.	
17/10/15	Completing camp & unty.	
18/10/15	Section inspecting new area & locating units	

WAR DIARY or INTELLIGENCE SUMMARY

Army Form C. 2118.

Hour, Date, Place	Summary of Events and Information	Remarks and references to Appendices
19/10/15 NOEUX LES MINES	In order to avoid delay during frequent change of position - a scheme is being initiated from today by which work at under a definite member of the section. No one responsible for following up & inspecting at the earliest opportunity after change of billet a carefully drawn up member of section will keep a record of all matters affecting the work of the unit in order to obviate two cases (these records will be examined each day by the C.O.). All work will be supervised by signed sergeants and all condition verify station needed.	
20/10/15 NOEUX LES MINES	L.C. Taylor wounded ack. Inspected area & billets of 7 (Bunn. Section) arrangement good, section carrying on routine work.	

Army Form C. 2118.

WAR DIARY
or
INTELLIGENCE SUMMARY
(Erase heading not required.)

Instructions regarding War Diaries and Intelligence Summaries are contained in F. S. Regs., Part II. and the Staff Manual respectively. Title pages will be prepared in manuscript.

Hour, Date, Place	Summary of Events and Information	Remarks and references to Appendices
21/10/15 NOEUX LES MINES	Found billets & unduly worn for section. Cleaning & changing over new billets. Squads inspecting units - kept three in trenches.	J.A.B.
22/10/15 "	Stores moved from cart to billet. Visited reserve billets with town major. Investigated case of S.F. amongst civil population & led area placed out of bounds. Section inspecting billets etc.	J.A.B.
23/10/15	Went over whole of this area with S.A.D.M.S. Arranged for work of section. Six men of 1 Regt. to be attached to division S.C. (476) at PHILOSOPHE for billets behind trenches. Vidence sent in me under Regt. BIRNIE.	J.A.B.
24/10/15	Vidence sent. Role in me at 47 for Interviewed wok for town major at Cage billet. Investigated complaint by 72 AC re manure etc.	J.A.B.

Army Form C. 2118.

WAR DIARY
or
INTELLIGENCE SUMMARY

(Erase heading not required.)

Hour, Date, Place	Summary of Events and Information	Remarks and references to Appendices
24/10/15 NOEUX LES MINES	Directions given re statement of nuisance	JHB
25/10/15 "	Sergt "BLENCH" & 1 man to PHILOSOPHE for inspection of billets of troops in action. Vidace set in use. Effects from water supply at FONTAIN DE BRAY investigated and report submitted. Routine work by section.	JHB
26/10/15	Vidace not handed over to San Sec 47 Div. Routine work at PHILOSOPHE & NOEUX LES MINES. Personnel inspection of ammunition at Café de Trouch, not water in action, capacity still very cold 2 days. Expended double nerorotin being conducted.	JHB
27/10/15	Routine work. Personnel inspection of camp, hotel keepers explained. Inspection of latrines etc held latrines etc into Town major.	JHB

1247 W 3290 500,000 (E) 8/14 J.B.C.&A. Forms/C. 2118/11.

Army Form C. 2118.

WAR DIARY
or
INTELLIGENCE SUMMARY
(Erase heading not required.)

Instructions regarding War Diaries and Intelligence Summaries are contained in F.S. Regs., Part II. and the Staff Manual respectively. Title pages will be prepared in manuscript.

Hour, Date, Place	Summary of Events and Information	Remarks and references to Appendices
28/10/15 NOEUX LES MINES	Interviewed Maj. BLENCH re work behind trenches. Being new troops to billets + at present little can be done.	
29/10/15	Section carried on routine inspections + reporting. Investigated case of paratyphoid 73 in A.g. + 16th H. Gave full directions to prevent spread. Inspected billets + sanitary arrangements of A.g. 16th H. and Royal Scots. — many improvements necessary. Long field recon necessary. Extr house inspection investigating causes of illness. Two cases of condensed milk being supplied with rations.	J.F.S.
30/10/15	Pay day. Routine work. Interviewed Town Major. A.A. + QMG. ADMS. CRE. DADOS + Engineer re scheme for latrines in the town. Waited for necessary material between C.O. S.S. + 74. re critical civil emergence — completed. Section meeting. Pereval unit to further order for latrines.	J.F.S.

31/10/15

Summarised but not copied

No. 32 Sanitary Section.

1915/16
October 1915.

X 32 San Se

WAR DIARY
or
INTELLIGENCE SUMMARY

Army Form C. 2118

Vol 3

CONFIDENTIAL DIARY

32nd Sanitary Section

att'd 15th Division

OCTOBER 1915

(reconstructed as far as possible from notes
to replace original lost + felt)

J.P. Hawkes (Capt. RAMC (T))
OC S Se 32

WAR DIARY
or
INTELLIGENCE SUMMARY

(Erase heading not required.)

Army Form C. 2118

Instructions regarding War Diaries and Intelligence Summaries are contained in F.S. Regs., Part II. and the Staff Manual respectively. Title Pages will be prepared in manuscript.

Place	Date	Hour	Summary of Events and Information	Remarks and references to Appendices
LA BUISSIERE	1.10.15		Troops moving. Section moved from MESDIGNEUIL to LA BUISSIERE. Have erected a camp established by 7 p.m. Section in tents.	JFF
"	2.10.15		Section engaged in putting camp in order. Also ventured inspection of troops resting. Some relaxation of sanitary discipline owing to section after the attack.	JFF
LAPUGNOY	3.10.15		Section moved from LABUSSIERE to LAPUGNOY. Have erected by 6 p.m. Established. Section in tents in field alongside station.	JFF
"	4.10.15		Camp put in order. Routine unit inspection commenced.	JFF
"	5.10.15		Routine inspection work of units extending from MARLES LES MINES to LILLERS. Special water duty men appointed. LAPUGNOY supplies tested. Scarcity of pumps along the stream, many polluted water food supply near railway crossing. Water & action accordingly.	JFF

Army Form C. 2118

WAR DIARY
or
INTELLIGENCE SUMMARY
(Erase heading not required.)

Instructions regarding War Diaries and Intelligence Summaries are contained in F. S. Regs., Part II. and the Staff Manual respectively. Title Pages will be prepared in manuscript.

Place	Date	Hour	Summary of Events and Information	Remarks and references to Appendices
LAPUGNOY	6.10.15		Special inspection of LILLERS district. Inspected of water supplies & routine inspection continues.	AMS
"	7.10.15		Special inspection of ALLOUAGNE district. Very few permanent sanitary arrangements. Routine inspection all new areas.	AMS
"	8.10.15		Special inspection of LAPUGNOY district. Notice board fixed to all potable water supplies in the area.	AMS
"	9.10.15		Squad detailed under Serg.t "BLENCH" for LILLERS area, the duties was two great to clean of satisfactory work.	AMS
"	10.10.15		Section resting	AMS
"	11.10.15		Routine inspection. LOZINGHEM & MARLES special inspection	AMS

WAR DIARY
or
INTELLIGENCE SUMMARY
(Erase heading not required.)

Army Form C. 2118

Place	Date	Hour	Summary of Events and Information	Remarks and references to Appendices
LAPUGNOY	12.10.15		Routine inspection. Inspection note that it is more difficult to keep units up to usual high standard of sanitary detail than is probably due to damage of drum reality fm enemy shelling. The big attack. LAPUGNOY especially inspected	[sgd]
"	13.10.15		Routine inspection units etc LILLERS district specially visited	[sgd]
"	14.10.15		Routine inspection ALLOUAGNE district specially visited	[sgd]
"	15.10.15		Routine inspection LILLERS agri-col region section	[sgd]
"	16.10.15		Section moved fm LAPUGNOY to NOEUX LES MINES Copelid by S fm Shelled infact & infact no damage to gotr/int d'abris to LAPUGNOY ext	[sgd]

WAR DIARY or INTELLIGENCE SUMMARY

Army Form C. 2118

Place	Date	Hour	Summary of Events and Information	Remarks and references to Appendices
NOEUX LES MINES	17.10.15		Capt at NOEUX LES MINES hut & adm Section in Ech: Hector heavy cold & deaf.	JPP
"	18.10.15		Routine inspection of area commenced. Inspection directed to examine huts & distribs: Interview with town mayor re unsatisfactory state of town as regards latrines, manure etc. Scheme submitted.	JPP
"	19.10.15		Routine inspection by section. Careful analysis of feeally area; for insanitary refuse etc revised & discussed with town mayor. Interview with divisional staff & visit to recent fighting & cabts.	JPP
"	20.10.15		Routine work & further details of sanitary scheme worked out.	JPP
"	21.10.15		Further efforts to report bywd routes sanitary work	JPP
"	22.10.15		"	JPP

Army Form C. 2118

WAR DIARY
or
INTELLIGENCE SUMMARY
(Erase heading not required.)

Instructions regarding War Diaries and Intelligence Summaries are contained in F. S. Regs., Part II and the Staff Manual respectively. Title Pages will be prepared in manuscript.

Place	Date	Hour	Summary of Events and Information	Remarks and references to Appendices
NOEUX-LES-MINES	23.10.15		Routine section work. Inspected water supply at FONTAIN-DE-BRAY. MOTELLES. Report submitted to ADMS. Section moved its billet — an infected house in main street of NOEUX, hut for room arrangement, cleaning & disinfection of cage shed at stables.	JTB
	24.10.15		Shed at stables thoroughly cleaned & disinfected, fatigue party supplied by Command. Routine infected work etc. elsewhere. Cyclist from OC. 72 RFA re manure dump near camp, also spy ? of RIDANGE ats agricultural guns billet. Cyclist investigated & steps taken to remedy.	JTB
	25.10.15		Serj. Black & 5 O.R. detailed for shed infected duties in PHILOSOPHE & district. Detail of 7 & 4 for at manning various billets in NOEUX specially infected. Cyclists & etc. of Sgt & C.	JTB

Army Form C. 2118

WAR DIARY
or
INTELLIGENCE SUMMARY
(Erase heading not required.)

Instructions regarding War Diaries and Intelligence Summaries are contained in F. S. Regs., Part II. and the Staff Manual respectively. Title Pages will be prepared in manuscript.

Place	Date	Hour	Summary of Events and Information	Remarks and references to Appendices
NOEUX-LES-MINES	26.10.15		Refitted crew of entire troops & trucks. Investigate & report by M.O. of unit.	
			Special investigation & report upon suitability of hastily built trestle & culverts for inclusion in sanitary scheme. Route work by members of sectn. Special attention being given to the question of rivets. Measurets of type proposed for extsd. crew constructed Cubical sectn. beats & exprmt. Pattn. with dry-y-plate & slating tile.	☒
"	27.10.15		Work connected with regard to new sanitary area. Site by closed. Huments & conversts to be alterd. by Engineer fatigue party. w/o with G.S. wagns. for Regt.	☒
"	28.10.15		Route sectn. work. Consult. with O.C. 9" D.S. /c. Plan subttd & approved.	☒

Army Form C. 2118

WAR DIARY
or
INTELLIGENCE SUMMARY
(Erase heading not required.)

Instructions regarding War Diaries and Intelligence Summaries are contained in F. S. Regs., Part II. and the Staff Manual respectively. Title Pages will be prepared in manuscript.

Place	Date	Hour	Summary of Events and Information	Remarks and references to Appendices
NOEUX-LES-MINES	29.10.16		Routine section work. Interview with O.C. No Signal Co re establishing investigators & infantry for care of practical telephone cables effected, units asked as far publicly as possible to return [illegible] to owner.	A/10
	30.10.16		Reply made. Interview with members of PHILOSOPHE S[illegible] Conductors of further section for routing returns.	A/10
	31.10.16		Section work.	C/10

1875 W: W593/826 1,000,000 4/15 J.B.C. &A. A.D.S.S./Forms/C.2118.

San: Sek: No: 32
tot. 4

D/7795

15/15 Hussein

Immarried but not esped

32 SAN. SECTION

Nov. 15

S/
Oct. 19.15

Army Form C. 2118

WAR DIARY
or
INTELLIGENCE SUMMARY
(Erase heading not required.)

Confidential

War Diary
Sanitary Section 32

November 1915.

J.F. Fawkes.
Capt. R.A.M.C.(T)
O.C. Sec. 32

Army Form C. 2118.

WAR DIARY
or
INTELLIGENCE SUMMARY
(Erase heading not required.)

Instructions regarding War Diaries and Intelligence Summaries are contained in F. S. Regs., Part II. and the Staff Manual respectively. Title pages will be prepared in manuscript.

Hour, Date, Place	Summary of Events and Information	Remarks and references to Appendices
1/11/15 MOEUX LES MINES	Interviewed Engineers re scheme for sanitary areas in the town. Their arrangements made and foundations of areas commenced. Section superintending the work also carrying on routine inspections.	For scheme see Appendix I
2/11/15 "	Reinforcement Pte HOLT joined section. Scheme in progress 2 G.S.W. for field stables 2 working parties from P.A. & trenchmen in Engineer carriery work in shelter for Latrine contr. half full & carcases, investigated complaints	JFB
3/11/15 "		JFB
4/11/15 "	Sqad from Philoso[?] sent against man hole station, investigated complaint re billets & lost matter adjusted. Routine work & scheme in progress. Serg't INCHLEY started on leave one HAVRE	JFB JFB

Army Form C. 2118.

WAR DIARY
or
INTELLIGENCE SUMMARY
(Erase heading not required.)

Hour, Date, Place	Summary of Events and Information	Remarks and references to Appendices
5/11/15 NOEUX LES MINES	Woodwork of three areas practically completed. Foundation for four areas in progress. Bricks being collected for ventilation. Billet census being made, lists of L/C TOPPING FITZGERALD & MAXWELL, with summary of sanitary condition. N.C.O. of section supervising various areas.	J.J.H.
6/11/15 "	Sanitary areas progressing well. Recent infection carried on supervision of areas etc. No fresh infection cases. Sickrate half list mostly mural cases.	J.J.H.
7/11/15 "	Section inspection. Investigated case of ENTERIC at HOUCHIN Des Orleans (KEITH) no sign of epidemic.	

WAR DIARY
or
INTELLIGENCE SUMMARY

Army Form C. 2118.

Hour, Date, Place	Summary of Events and Information	Remarks and references to Appendices
8/11/15 NOEUX LES MINES	Area practically used for Rotation. Routine inspection carried out & such formal measures in the town studied to refuse dump & latrines &c. no movement.	J.H. Barker
9/11/15	Area was started thoroughly. Inspection was not completed. Knock holds implant in rear of 72 R.F.A. (R.Enly) & Block hotel had sand rotary area also. Medical officers section engaged with inspections & supervision. Recent drain emptied.	J.F.B.
10/11/15	Routine work for section. Limited visit of latrines &c. in infection to A.D.M.S. P.C. Buster out to 8 OM₃R – later detail plate 1st mod sanitary areas with O.C. g. field P.C.	J.F.B.
11/11/15	Routine work. Nothing special to report.	J.F.B.
12/11/15	Pay day. Routine inspections. Four areas in partial use.	J.F.B.

WAR DIARY
or
INTELLIGENCE SUMMARY

(Erase heading not required.)

Army Form C. 2118.

Hour, Date, Place	Summary of Events and Information	Remarks and references to Appendices
13/11/15 NOEUX LES MINES	44 Bg⁴⁵ to trenches 45" to NOEUX LES MINES RUDICOURT, VERQUIN, Infantry of Reels Cpt G antger troops, report on any left in unsatisfactory condition. Resett of war to incoming troops. Investigate of anual explod to Reels. Infected areas will. Coppell to the Reels. L.C. Burber returned. A.D.M.S + D.A.D.M.S. Section meeting.	JHB.
14/11/15 15/11/15	Routine work. 2nd Sanitary officer of Div. (what will probably take over the area) to be wind round sanitary situation etc. explained scheme. L.Cpl. Kelley returned from leave. Went round various type of Reets with A.Dn.	JHB.
16/11/15	Fatigue party returned fr. (Cafe de Paris) left in bad condition (F + gardens) to see if this will take Went with A.D.m. S to area the road. Paw C. Dudg is to North gate opposite	JHB.

Army Form C. 2118.

WAR DIARY
or
INTELLIGENCE SUMMARY.
(Erase heading not required.)

Instructions regarding War Diaries and Intelligence Summaries are contained in F.S. Regs, Part II. and the Staff Manual respectively. Title pages will be prepared in manuscript.

Hour, Date, Place	Summary of Events and Information	Remarks and references to Appendices
17/11/15 NOEUX LES MINES	Routine inspection was performed into Cpt Lemoine a polorica. Large detonator found. killed all country are a the Town.	JFH
18/11/15 "	Routine work. Refresher in week cestegrading for Battalion started to have uphow, were to into will.	JFH
19/11/15 "	twenty odd saw back explant & adjutant Capsland is in Su has been hospitali. Showed 1st Su chiefs at fort. All notify Crations he is Su has received last working out Sergeant Capsy takes Billet CH & asketh another instigated own of Party [illeg] R & 6 [illeg]	JFH
20/11/15 "	Routine work, sincery Area allotted to new unit.	JFH
21/11/15 "	Section resting.	

1247 W 3299 200,000 (E) 8/14 J.R.C. & A. Forms/C.2118/11.

WAR DIARY
or
INTELLIGENCE SUMMARY
(Erase heading not required.)

Army Form C. 2118.

Hour, Date, Place	Summary of Events and Information	Remarks and references to Appendices
22/11/15 NOEUX LES MINES	Visited PHILOSOPHE & FERVELLES & obtained from T. R.F.A. Denmark supply of fork on shelter one bay constructed. Every country work I.P.B. & MAZINGARBE. Visited DROUVIN & saw up Fouquland B. & Gelet. Capt & Cupboat is numerous billets & billeted of staff & notice to ready gun and section.	JHJ
23/11/15 "	On informed class of men in RUE DE LA BOURSE. Route inspection. Saw Lieut & other of section in DROUVIN	JHJ SPO
24/11/15 "	Week change of infantry activity. Nothing to report. Made arrangements	JHJ
25/11/15 26/11/15	Section charged billets to DROUVIN. Investigated complaint re billets left in bad condition by 10 Gordon. Billets in very bad state. Notice sent to Coy O.C.	JHJ

WAR DIARY
or
INTELLIGENCE SUMMARY

Army Form C. 2118

Place	Date	Hour	Summary of Events and Information	Remarks and references to Appendices
DROUVIN	27/11/15		Sector arrangement effected. Visits to neighbourhood inspected. Visits noted.	9776
"	28/11/15		Personal inspection of area now occupied by the division with D.A.D.M.S. of 12th Division for returns. Collection of statistics left at Mondicourt by 12th Division for returns.	9776
"	29/11/15		Routine inspection carried out by the section.	9776
"	30/11/15		Scheme to cover Kings stay of 14 days in district. Area divided into inspection areas. Arrangements made for Sgnd. S/10 a Sgn. Bland to be elected at SAILLY LE BOURSE	9776

WAR DIARY or INTELLIGENCE SUMMARY

Hour, Date, Place: Appendix I

Summary of Events and Information

Scheme for sanitary areas in towns & on lines.

The need for some definite scheme

Billeted in the town where there are no people available for its upkeep & refuse, the sanitation often has failed nearly all available prompts are not available but the winter months. Practically every available area in any shape available is used as an interior latrine. This is had both from the standpoint of military hygiene & military discipline. Lack of such facilities is a contributing factor to ill health among the troops.

The scheme, which is capable of expansion provides for the area carefully selected after examination of the various billeting area allotted to Battalions of the XV Division in Nov: 1915. Some of these sanitary areas are for definite units, one for public use, each supplies latrine accommodation, urinals and a destructor, capable of dealing with refuse, and in certain areas with excreta as well. Each area has a supplementary trenching ground for all excreta which cannot be burnt. Each area will have a sanitary policeman – from the town Majors staff – in charge who will be responsible for the incineration, latrine pails and other details. This will normally be worked daily by a N.C.O from the Sanitary section of the Division using the area, and the sanitary personnel of the unit to whom each area is allotted. It will be worked daily after the movement of troops be expected to give assistance. The trucks system will be applied to the larger areas having so pails all the smaller areas 15. There will be two mine pits, used alternately and an incinerator either of the open or closed type, the latter will deal with excreta as well as refuse.

WAR DIARY or INTELLIGENCE SUMMARY

Army Form C. 2118.

(Erase heading not required.)

Instructions regarding War Diaries and Intelligence Summaries are contained in F. S. Regs., Part II. and the Staff Manual respectively. Title pages will be prepared in manuscript.

Hour, Date, Place	Summary of Events and Information	Remarks and references to Appendices

The huts will stand upon a slag foundation and will be covered in by a canvas and felt shelter. A pole near will be provided, on the account and the pools & places too close to the track wall of the shelter. The pole must fit as closely as convenient to the upper edge of the pail.

The urine pits will be of the closes and filled in types, and to provide with funnels or troughs.

The close urinals will have a sloping plate above the flue upon which excreta matter will be placed. It will be so constructed that the fumes from the sun furnace through the flame of the incinerator will so pass through.

Care of latrines. It will be the duty of the sanitary policeman to see that the incinerator is carefully stoked and the pails frequently emptied. Pails will be kitted over with dead daily and cleaned by filling with each at the trenched area. Units will take their refuse to the incinerator three daily. They will be informed to which area the refuse is to be taken & brown will be made for doing the refuse until it can be burnt.

Units will be notified of their latrine area as soon as possible after arrival.

Suggested rules for control. (1) Battalions taking up billets will be allowed as soon as possible after arrival to their latrine area. (2) NCO's in charge will call latrines will see that the men use their latrines are to be kept clear. (3) Notice will state 1 hour before the incineration to what refuse is to be taken. These will hung up in each billet into which all refuse will be thrown. The container is made will be removed to the incinerator twice a day, the contents burnt, and the pails replaced. (4) Sanitary horaetal of latrines will again be placed in charge and to batalens duty. (5) Every Battalion commander will see to him that the rules of sanitary discipline & hygiene must be kept clear by the occupants of the billets.

Signature (6) See ahead roadway

Form C 2118/15
1247 W 3259 200,000 (E) 5/14 J.R.C. & A.

WAR DIARY
or
INTELLIGENCE SUMMARY
(Erase heading not required.)

Army Form C. 2118

Place	Date	Hour	Summary of Events and Information	Remarks and references to Appendices
			Duties of permanent sanitary police. (1) To see no damage is done, and nothing removed. (2) To keep areas clean, tidy. (3) To empty pails & lids systematically. (No pail must be allowed to be more than half full.) (4) To sprinkle chloride of lime from funnels of urine for than half full. (5) To see that urinals is carefully closed & burn all refuse. (6) To bury ashes, tins etc. after cremation. (7) To remove any slag when has been fouled & replace. (8) To keep pails clean. Suggested time table for policemen on duty. 8.30 Any urines for the day. 9-11 Empty urine pails. Duty area Burn refuse (see that incinerate is burning well) 1-2.30 Duty up (no paper must be left lying about) Replace any soiled slag, attend to urinals. Empty pails if necessary. 4-5 (or until finished) Duty up Empty lean ale pails. See that all refuse is burnt, pails or urinals burnt. N/B Any loss of pails or structural damage to be reported at once to Town Major.	

Sou: Sect: 32
Vol: 5

12/7928

14/5/21
15/5/21

F1 2541

December 1915

Summarised but not copied

Army Form C. 2118.

WAR DIARY
or
INTELLIGENCE SUMMARY

(Erase heading not required.)

Instructions regarding War Diaries and Intelligence Summaries are contained in F. S. Regs., Part II. and the Staff Manual respectively. Title pages will be prepared in manuscript.

Hour, Date, Place	Summary of Events and Information	Remarks and references to Appendices
	CONFIDENTIAL DIARY DEC. 1915 SANITARY SEC. 32 of 2nd Lowland Sanitary Co. c/o Dev xi B.E.F. J.P.Hawkes (Cpl. N.M.C.(T)) O.C. San. Sec. 32	

Army Form C. 2118

WAR DIARY
or
INTELLIGENCE SUMMARY
(Erase heading not required.)

Instructions regarding War Diaries and Intelligence Summaries are contained in F.S. Regs., Part II. and the Staff Manual respectively. Title Pages will be prepared in manuscript.

Place	Date	Hour	Summary of Events and Information	Remarks and references to Appendices
DROUVIN	1/2/17		General inspection of complete area. "L'C" Sanitary Section in VAUDRICOURT. Inspection of VERQUIN shew that it is unfavorable to make use of area. Latrines etc fit in of D area awaiting erection. Park have been removed & "area manned" every to look of references during movement of division; roads, mud, making of waresites & latrines are to be perfectly used.	SM
"	2/2/17		Sjt." BLENCH by squad of sams — (L.C. made Baths, Trestles, Hardy inspection. O'Brien, Wigley & Dr. HOLT) to LA BOURSE for spare inspection; returned by 46 F.a.	SM
"	3/2/17		Found infants VAUDRICOURT, VERQUIN & 46 F.a. Visited VERQUIN & district. Doctor went going in cold. Lasting conveniences being made use of throughout district except area 2 at VERQUIN which cannot be used owing to have been.	SM
"	4/2/17		Visited HESDIGNEUIL area.	SM
"	5/2/17		Sector sanitary. Visited LA BOURSE & SAILLY LA BOURSE. District work of sections.	SM

Army Form C. 2118

WAR DIARY
or
INTELLIGENCE SUMMARY
(Erase heading not required.)

Instructions regarding War Diaries and Intelligence Summaries are contained in F.S. Regs., Part II. and the Staff Manual respectively. Title Pages will be prepared in manuscript.

Place	Date	Hour	Summary of Events and Information	Remarks and references to Appendices
JROUVIN	6/12/15	—	Visited A.C.S. Verquin. Routine work by section. Lorry – slight accident – admound cyclist said to have been knocked off his bicycle. Known to have been close shut out in front of car. Injury to charge of needles during. The driver showed lack of judgment, attended to.	JAH
"	7/12/15		Visited Routine work by section.	JAH
"	8/12/15		Nothing special to report. Visited LILLERS.	JAH
"	9/12/15		Visited LILLERS re beds etc. Went not satisfactory. Arranged to have lorry ordered by O.C. I.A.M.	JAH
"	10/12/15		Visited field cookers. Arranged for DAILY visits to regt. in 110/15. Routine inspection carried out. Reports satisfactory but weather conditions very adverse. Pay day. Sergt. BLENCH & squad reported.	JAH
"	11/12/15		Visited LILLERS & completed arrangement.	JAH

1875 Wt. W593/826 1,000,000 4/15 J.B.C. & A. A.D.S.S./Forms/C.2118.

Army Form C. 2118

WAR DIARY
or
INTELLIGENCE SUMMARY
(Erase heading not required.)

Place	Date	Hour	Summary of Events and Information	Remarks and references to Appendices
DROUVIN	13/1/16		Visited NOEUX LES MINES Sanitary Schn. working well. Tried to obtain voiture or lorry for M.O. unable to do so. took a walk. Route inspection & slogging return by fields	Appx
"	14/1/16		Advance party & two book shelter to LILLERS	Appx
LILLERS	15/1/16		Section moved by rail to LILLERS. Start in order. Billets cleaned	Appx
"	16/1/16		Arrang sanitary details of billet etc. Inspection of new Sanitary lectures to Officers at relief of No Section relieved of the 19th G.R. gun by...	Appx
"	17/1/16		Inspection of LILLERS RAIMBERT BURBURE. Pumil put to remove fats of one with ADMS	Appx
"	18/1/16		Carrayes for latrine, sanitary squads to 22, 23 & 24 Gnd of 10 & AVEHEL with Coy "S" Ranch. To distribute of work see appendix	Appx
"	19/1/16		Visited Rombent - BURBURE Lecturing	Appx Appx

WAR DIARY
or
INTELLIGENCE SUMMARY

(Erase heading not required.)

Army Form C. 2118.

Hour, Date, Place	Summary of Events and Information	Remarks and references to Appendices
20/12/15 LILLERS.	Visited Laundry (Bn) at ALLOUAGNE with D.A.D.M.S. Dentist inspected Count in E.9 section. Periodical inspection of 3 Battalions in LILLERS Billets Latrines water supply etc	JJJ Barker
21/12/15	Investigation as to causes which give rise to Throat infections in men at front. Out of Bounds for troops. Lecture to sanitary personnel of 46th Brigade.	JJJ
22/12/15	Investigated action re measles caused by means. Gen section of N.C.O. (C. Hoart & town major) & Veterans & Brigadier mgr. 45 bgde re Sub-of night and in LILLERS. Advice on any thing. Inspected billets of A & Buts Regt (Bunde) Latrines accommodation provided at rest home Lectures to sanitary men at ALLOUAGNE Dental inspection	JJJ
23/12/15	Personal inspection with 9.0.B.A.S. at BURBURG of 8 K.O.S.R.	JJJ

Army Form C. 2118.

WAR DIARY
or
INTELLIGENCE SUMMARY

(Erase heading not required.)

Instructions regarding War Diaries and Intelligence Summaries are contained in F.S. Regs., Part II. and the Staff Manual respectively. Title pages will be prepared in manuscript.

Hour, Date, Place	Summary of Events and Information	Remarks and references to Appendices
24/12/15 LILLERS	Lecture to sanitary personel of units at AUCHEL. Routine inspections. Report shew satisfactory sanitary conditions in all units.	JJHS
25/12/15 "		JJHS
26/12/15 "	Section resting.	
27/12/15 "	Inspection work resumed. Personal visit to RAIMBERT by of 10th Jo. Rfle. Found post could be fixed. Interview with medical officer. Horses a too mange. is case of J.I. typhoid nurse block transport of Royal Scots Lucerne. Saw adjutant.	JJHS
28/12/15 "	Routine inspections satisfactory but all sanitary work much hampered by waterlogged state of country.	JJHS

WAR DIARY
or
INTELLIGENCE SUMMARY

Army Form C. 2118.

Hour, Date, Place	Summary of Events and Information	Remarks and references to Appendices
LILLERS. 29/12/15	Routine inspection by section. Route march to HURIONVILLE (bicyclists) ALLOUAGNE (7 Coms & Bloodhounds) returning report upon 10 pryd rifle interview report upon + have LE Tupping out + have Cyclists analysis of daily reports - saltpetre	J.H.Bauke
30/12/15	Lecture et school of instruction GOSNAY a Sanitation Routine work by section	J.H.Bauke J.H.Dawkes
31/12/15	" " During the next period schedule work has been in autre taken with lectus to Sanitary squads + officers also systematic inspection of all units	J.H.Bauke

Army Form C. 2118.

WAR DIARY
or
INTELLIGENCE SUMMARY
(Erase heading not required.)

Instructions regarding War Diaries and Intelligence Summaries are contained in F. S. Regs., Part II. and the Staff Manual respectively. Title pages will be prepared in manuscript.

Hour, Date, Place	Summary of Events and Information	Remarks and references to Appendices
18/12/15	Distribution of Sanitary Section awell Lights under Capt Bleach.	Apphdr 1
	Lance Corpl Collins — 13th R.F.A.	
	— 15th Div Amm. Col.	
	Lance Corpl Graham — 91st Royal Engineers	
	— Div. Train	
	Lance Corpl Booth — 70 R.F.A	
	— 71 R.F.A	
	Lance Corpl O'Connor — 10th Scottish Rifles	
	— 12 Highland Light Infy	
	Lance Corpl Wrigley — 1/4 Suffolks (T)	
	— 9th Gordons	
	Lance Corpl Maxwell — 10th Gordons	
	— 74th Royal Engineers	
	Lance Corpl Topping — 9th Royal Highlanders	
	— 4th Camerons	

Army Form C. 2118.

WAR DIARY
or
INTELLIGENCE SUMMARY
(Erase heading not required.)

Hour, Date, Place	Summary of Events and Information	Remarks and references to Appendices
	Cellar Squad under Staff Sgt MacLeod.	Appendix I

	Lance Corpl Brodie 7th Royal Scots two.
	    " Burker 6th Camerons.
	    " Emmett 11th Argyll & Suth.
	                   13th Royal Scots
	    " Hardy 7th K.O.S.B
	                   8th K.O.S.B
	    " Standidge Div. Cavalry
	    " " Cyclists
	
	All points to be reported upon.
	Special attention to:-
	① Treatment of water - report in detail on every unit
	② Accessibility of urine pits latrines
	     (b) Latrines (b) Cesspools (muddy etc)
	③ Condition of Water Cart
	④ Careful survey of billeting conditions	

San: Sect: 32
Vol 6

15

15th Division

F/254/2

32 SAN. SECTION

Jan 1916

WAR DIARY
or
INTELLIGENCE SUMMARY

Army Form C. 2118.

(Erase heading not required.)

SANITARY SEC 32
2ⁿᵈ LONDON SANITARY CO

CONFIDENTIAL WAR DIARY

January 1916.
Vol.

FM Saunders
Capt N.ᶻ.M.C (ST)
OC San Sec 32.

Army Form C. 2118.

WAR DIARY
or
INTELLIGENCE SUMMARY

(Erase heading not required.)

Instructions regarding War Diaries and Intelligence Summaries are contained in F. S. Regs., Part II. and the Staff Manual respectively. Title pages will be prepared in manuscript.

Hour, Date, Place	Summary of Events and Information	Remarks and references to Appendices
LILLERS. 1/1/16	Section carrying out routine work. All guard duty waterlogged owing to continued rain and sanitary work as usual have improved.	G.T. Hawkes
" 2/1/16	Section resting. I gave lecture at BURBURE on the scheme "Hughes" to machine gun officers of 46th Brigade. Read out of instr'n re ALLOWANCE.	G.T. Hawkes
" 3/1/16	Routine work. Went with A.D.M.S. to AUCHEL. Interview at headquarters re distribution of section during divisional route march.	G.T. Hawkes
" 4/1/16	Lee arrangements made for divisional exercise. In order to make full use of the railway sect. the following scheme has been adopted. Section split up amongst various units of division so as far as possible the men per unit were allocated upon sanitary & hygiene of marching during the march. One of the section's attention to be paid to flooring huts.	

Army Form C. 2118.

WAR DIARY
or
INTELLIGENCE SUMMARY
(Erase heading not required.)

Hour, Date, Place	Summary of Events and Information	Remarks and references to Appendices
LILLERS. 5/1/16	(1) Sanitary precaus made during short halts. (2) " muddy belt (?) in going into (3) " Billets note especially how and fight aired latines etc are in use. (4) Use made of water carts during march (5) Whether indicements drinking from ponds. Also any other observations which may seem to be of certain importance. Reinforced their units during the day will " anding in state" never stay from serious duties. Section took during the evening. For distribution see appendix 1	J.F.Cooke Appendix A

WAR DIARY
or
INTELLIGENCE SUMMARY

Army Form C. 2118.

Hour, Date, Place	Summary of Events and Information	Remarks and references to Appendices
Appendix 1	Distribution of Sanitary rectus 3x during	
	13th Divisional exercises	
	2/Lt A.P.M.S.	O.C. section
	8. H.Q.	Lance Cpl Townsend Sick
	4th Brigade	Serjt Bland L/Cpl Pelham
	5th Royal Highlanders	L/Cpl Fitzgerald L/Cpl Rimmer
	6th Seaforth Highlanders	L/Cpl Partridge
	7th Gordons	L/Cpl Maxwell Nurses
	8th Gordons	L/Cpl Hardy Lce Serj Jones
	45th Brigade	Pte Prior
	6th Cameron Highlanders	Pte Peacock
	7th Cameron Highlanders	Pte Proctor
	8th [?] Highlanders	L/Cpl Brooke Pte Plows
	A & S Highlanders	L/Cpl Emmett
	46th Brigade	R. [?]
		Lce Serj Whalley L Serj Bunn
	7th K.O.Y.L.I.	L/Cpl Wrigley Sgt Tuffing
	10. Scottish Rifles	Pte Hull
	12. H.L.I.	L/Cpl O'Connor
	4. Suffolks	L/Cpl Colline Actg. N.C.O.C.
	7. Ampere R.F.A.	tealm Pte Wed
	7. D.I.A	
		Away & shown notion in car to L.L.G.R.S.

Army Form C. 2118.

WAR DIARY
or
INTELLIGENCE SUMMARY

(Erase heading not required.)

Instructions regarding War Diaries and Intelligence
Summaries are contained in F. S. Regs., Part II.
and the Staff Manual respectively. Title pages
will be prepared in manuscript.

Hour, Date, Place	Summary of Events and Information	Remarks and references to Appendices
5/1/16. LILLERS & ERNY ST JULIEN	Divisional route march. Sanitary section marching with unit as arranged. H.Q. to ERNY ST JULIEN. Section enabling formenelle garage road about 15 klmts. O.C. in see with ADMS	JTB
6/1/16 ERNY ST JULIEN	Divisional exercises. Heavy wind & rain all day. Field ambulances with ADMS during day.	JTB
7/1/16 LILLERS	Orders of exercises read room fm midday. LILLERS Sqd returned to LILLERS. AUCHEL Sqd returned to AUCHEL.	JTB
8/1/16 "	Nothing special to report. Section dealing with Sanitation of march, compiling reports etc	JTB
9/1/16 "	Orders re return to NOEUX LES MINES. Section making	JTB
10/1/16 "	Section. Visited "NOEUX LES MINES" arrangements made for billets. Routine inspection work.	JTB

1247 W 3299 200,000 (E) 8/14 J.R.C.&A. Forms/C. 2118/11.

Army Form C. 2118.

WAR DIARY
or
INTELLIGENCE SUMMARY
(Erase heading not required.)

Instructions regarding War Diaries and Intelligence Summaries are contained in F. S. Regs, Part II. and the Staff Manual respectively. Title pages will be prepared in manuscript.

Hour, Date, Place	Summary of Events and Information	Remarks and references to Appendices
LILLERS 11/1/16.	Visited 46 Fd. Group to find bury on 13th inst. One of party had a report of 1/3 D.F.A. returns rectitude, field ammunition sent to ride & officer. (1st section case a dummy notified for 4 weeks.) Section out to continue work.	JHB
12/1/16	1 Sergeant to NOEUX LES MINES to get a truck with our company workshop & ceiling done.	JHB
12/1/16	Sergt Blead to MAZINGARBE. Rec End of section stores called to NIEUX. Permits made ALLOUAGNE to multiple coys of party had MARLES LES MINES. Sealed from RAIMBERT. Water supply sent of 10th Division BURBURE. 1" ROP R. Section work & suspension for more section moved to NOEUX LES MINES	JHB
13/1/16 14/1/16	"	JHB
NOEUX LES MINES 15/1/16	Anxious heat work on Mines German exploded mine	JHB

1247 W 3290 200,000 (E) 8/14 J.B.C. & A. Forms/C. 2118/11.

Army Form C. 2118.

WAR DIARY
or
INTELLIGENCE SUMMARY
(Erase heading not required.)

Instructions regarding War Diaries and Intelligence Summaries are contained in F. S. Regs., Part II. and the Staff Manual respectively. Title pages will be prepared in manuscript.

Hour, Date, Place	Summary of Events and Information	Remarks and references to Appendices
NOEUX-LES-MINES 16/1/16	Section resting	
" 17/1/16	Case of Enteric in Noeux Les Mines investigated. Cases in estaminet from Head of 10th Bn. Case of measles in Convryght Bn in Rangold. Cafés, sheds, beet sugar station visited.	SHS
" 18/1/16	Drainage of 8 & 9 ms in stat changing colour to be investigated. Routine inspection carried on in new area. Disinfector carried out at 45 fc. ? Diphtheria investigation & cases in affect in readiness. Condition of Ordnance Pad; Billet at Heidigneul. Routine work.	SHS
" 19/1/16	Further disinfection of large billet at Heidigneul. Noeux selected for Steam Fumigator. Investigation of infected latrines at Mazingarbo should case to be one of ptomaine poisoning.	SHS

WAR DIARY or INTELLIGENCE SUMMARY

Army Form C. 2118.

Hour, Date, Place	Summary of Events and Information	Remarks and references to Appendices
NOEUX-LES-MINES		
20/1/16	Sanitary areas of NOEUX-LES-MINES inspected	JPB
21/1/16	71st NFA Special inspection. Scheme for street cleaning prepared & Staff Serg'nt Clarke & gully boiled & theatre cold.	JPB
22/1/16	Further survey of gulleys & drains etc. re. treatment. Registration re. treatment.	
	Routine inspection & inspection of sulphur chambers continued.	JPB
23/1/16	Eyesight tests at 111 F.A. surrounded by Sergt Runie.	
24/1/16	Farms & trans'gres tested. Examination for enteric fever & plan re. same re-opened. Special care re re-opening.	JPB
25/1/16	Routine work. "	JPB
26/1/16	Examination of routine work & special agencies.	JPB
27/1/16	Investigation of nuisance & rem'l of YMCA huts. Seed of Sanitary accommodation. Routine work	JPB

Army Form C. 2118.

WAR DIARY
or
INTELLIGENCE SUMMARY
(Erase heading not required.)

Hour, Date, Place	Summary of Events and Information	Remarks and references to Appendices
NOEUX-LES-MINES		
28/1/16	Enfrey stagnant water for cholern near 2 "? Reclamation.	HHS
29/1/16	Reconnaissance carried out at junction of BETHUNE DROUVIN road. Investigate of sanitary area + general sanitation at NOEUX LES MINES + MAZINGARBE. Interview with town mayor of both areas. Completion of special infection at water. " " Refuse. Submitted for analysis.	HHS
	Sech. Disinfect. + cleaning of headquarters office. Sech. ruling.	HHS
30/1/16	Routine inspection. Supervision of road cleaning. Investigation of complaints re broken detour. Interview town mayor re future arrival of troops.	HHS
31/1/16	Investigated available quartering of troops at VERQUIN.	HHanh

15th Div.

32nd Army Section

Feb 1916

32 Sanitary Section

Vol VII

WAR DIARY
or
INTELLIGENCE SUMMARY

CONFIDENTIAL WAR DIARY

SANITARY SECTION. 32

att 15" Div.

February 1916

J.H. Lambroe
Capt. R.a.m.c. (T)
O.C. San Sec 32

WAR DIARY
or
INTELLIGENCE SUMMARY
(Erase heading not required.)

Army Form C. 2118

Place	Date	Hour	Summary of Events and Information	Remarks and references to Appendices
NOEUX LES MINES	1/2/16		Paybook. Interview c̄ C.R.E. re latrine scheme for Y.M.C.A. huts. Inspection of all sanitary area in NOEUX LES MINES. Routine work.	JHB
"	2/2/16		Serg. Burns colour/rod cleaning. Inspected Pithead with Serg "BLENCH". Interview with C.R.E. re new area of Y.M.C.A. hut. Inspected various pumps in villages. Lecture doing routine work. Throughout is trapt been heated.	JHB
"	3/4/16		Completed 2nd cleaning at MAISNARD & course by Serg. BLENCH. There is still one cholera latrine, all else is left. Must explain of its very effects are left. Inspected R.A.E. 76, 7, 7, 73, + Divisional Cavalry at VERQUIN VAUDRICOURT. DROUVIN. Sanitary arrangements quite satisfactory. Except for two rubbish heaps near Billets. Interview C.O. These will be cleared.	JHB
"	4/1/16		O-dinant of Billet - RUE BASSÉ with sunken latrine in Billet. Saw Town Major who took it cleared. Pr. HOLT model Grease Gpit (infantry). Defice defect in RUE D'ARRAS cleared. Office infection. Five infection. Hospital. Several outbreaks of Billets. Routine inspection in progress.	JHB

WAR DIARY
or
INTELLIGENCE SUMMARY

Army Form C. 2118

Place	Date	Hour	Summary of Events and Information	Remarks and references to Appendices
NOEUX LES MINES	5/2/16		Inspection of Reets by G.O.C. Orders drafted re sanitation of Reets. New hut - army pattern 1914 hut inspected. Works work proceeding.	S.H.D.
"	6/2/16		Noted many mistakes in new latrine area.	
"	7/2/16		Commenced latrine area behind G.M.C.A. hut. Inspection of Reets received by Lt. Curtis. Report 6.40 re neglect of fat of Pte. L. Scott. Also to m.o. re his Reets left by C.P.S. Snellum. At S.H.Q. 13. Good all case of neg. Bat. dealt with.	A.F.Y.
"	8/2/16		Works work carried on. Experiment with new syphon trumpeter closures, receptacle not satisfactory, perfect condition. Burnt & styled receptacle contents. Latrine are burning. Latrine party from 4/5 field amb. Works work twenty satisfactory. Now cleaning mud reg. and irregular fatigue parties to dig out water army to P and out tries dry. (cemet.)	

WAR DIARY
or
INTELLIGENCE SUMMARY

Army Form C. 2118

Place	Date	Hour	Summary of Events and Information	Remarks and references to Appendices
NOEUX LES MINES	9/2/16		Inspection with ADMS of MAZINGARBE, PHILOSOPHE areas. Saturday crept in commanding position of what will be chief "check line" better to turn over with. Drainage effects satisfactory. Inspection of new huts just erected, incidents partially completed. Latrine seats needing — 3 tray exame filled the majority of jalopa bagpig charles. A few taken away in field of clothing removed. Fungi shaped receptacle worked well, further experiments tomorrow with 6 huts expense. Lecture to O.C. officers at school of instruction.	JJJ.A
NOEUX	10/2/16		Further experiments with Fungi style stoves. Eggs taken after free 2 hrs exposure. Placed in hen bag 2 mm — fresh. Faecal infection work. Lectures structure progressing, frame tops etc. for Y.M.C.A. over. Double work.	J.J.S
	11/2/16		New latrine area completed. Recruits being well fed.	
	12/2/16		Lecture to O.C. to new officers of 46th Brigade in sanitation. R.E.C. lecture area atout the hue. Experimental hen egg (10.2.16) hatched out. Chicks & hens expose in jalofer chalae not different sufficient & use, infection of 9° latent & heated & used.	J.J.S

Army Form C. 2118

WAR DIARY
or
INTELLIGENCE SUMMARY
(Erase heading not required.)

Instructions regarding War Diaries and Intelligence Summaries are contained in F.S. Regs., Part II. and the Staff Manual respectively. Title Pages will be prepared in manuscript.

Place	Date	Hour	Summary of Events and Information	Remarks and references to Appendices
NOEUX LES MINES	13/2/16		Section routine. Off billet where measles case had occurred. Disinfection of staff dugt of all areas in NOEUX LES MINES.	777
"	14/2/16		Inspection with Tn Mgn re roads. Latrines etc. Routine inspection of carts. Reports by medical of section. General state of town extreme to the mullet. Lee gas what fonds at NOEUX LES MINES. a lecture to refer into no of empty ground occupied by the train. Routine work of section.	777
"	15/4/16		Commenced measles behind recreation room. Le Dude readed to report is all reports satisfactory	777
"	16/4/16		Inspection of MAZINGARBE PHILOSOPHE area (funnel). Rest pole clearing from the west. Routine work of section. Inspected timber in the northern section with mgr Logan of 60 divison. Inspection of certain areas in NOEUX LES MINES.	777
"	17/2/16		Staines with brigade mgn of 44" brigade re water for a unit duty man killed 47 f a to two disinfection cases	777
"	18/2/16		Gr Wheel Parade. Completed arrangements for measles room	777
"	19/2/16		Staff conf. of O.C. a area. Routine work.	777

Army Form C. 2118

WAR DIARY
or
INTELLIGENCE SUMMARY
(Erase heading not required.)

Instructions regarding War Diaries and Intelligence Summaries are contained in F. S. Regs., Part II. and the Staff Manual respectively. Title Pages will be prepared in manuscript.

Place	Date	Hour	Summary of Events and Information	Remarks and references to Appendices
NOEUX LES MINES	20/2/16		Handed over c/o of 40 Div. on sanitary returned. Sect. units.	JFS
	21/2/16		New arrival felt fit in case 7 commenced. Arrangements made for dealing with the Sanitation formed infected points of 46 Brigade & 47 field ambulances. Routine inspection by section.	JFS
"	22/2/16		Bn inspection of billets etc more. Continuation of new work entailed, also clearing of yard at Café Bellevue. Work interfered with by heavy fall of snow. Pay Parade 4 P.M.	
			Investigation of case of measles amongst civilian population at PERCHIN & refugt. Routine work. Church of Avenue duchef. MAZINGARBE opened as training centre PHILOSOPHE CEE. Infection with ADMS of MAZINGARBE in perfect condition. Sanitary arrangements	JFS
"	23/2/16		Snow falling & hard frost.	
"	24/2/16		Routine work. Lecture in "Sanitation" to O.C. section of the School of huts work in Arias road. Disinfection of fifty billets.	JFS
"	25/2/16		Much snow & frost. Routine sectional work.	JFS

Army Form C. 2118

WAR DIARY
or
INTELLIGENCE SUMMARY
(Erase heading not required.)

Instructions regarding War Diaries and Intelligence Summaries are contained in F. S. Regs., Part II. and the Staff Manual respectively. Title Pages will be prepared in manuscript.

Place	Date	Hour	Summary of Events and Information	Remarks and references to Appendices
NOEUX LES MINES	26/2/16		Complete inspection of billets & NOEUX LES MINES & VC section. Billets now occupied by 7th & 8th KOSB very satisfactory, especially the latter.	APP
	27/2/16		Shed now in the ground interfering with sanitation work. Section resting.	APP
	28/2/16		Return to central mementos & sectional inspection work & sectional Number inspection of VERDUN. Satisfactory.	APP
	29/2/16		Fennell inspection of NOEUX LES MINES with A.D.M.S. Sale. Inspection of billets & now mementos. Return caused in to man mementos. Emerg'y for dealing with numerous & two billets good.	APP

1875 W: W593/826 1,000,000 4/15 J.B.C. & A. A.D.S.S./Forms/C. 2118.

WAR DIARIES

of

32nd Sanitary Section - 15th Division

for the months of

March and April 1916

WAR DIARY
or
INTELLIGENCE SUMMARY

Army Form C. 2118

32 mS
Jan Sie
Vol 8
15 Da

CONFIDENTIAL DIARY

SANITARY SECTION 32

Attached 15th Div B.E.F

March 1916.

Herbert Sanders
Cpt.
OC San Sec 32.

WAR DIARY
or
INTELLIGENCE SUMMARY

(Erase heading not required.)

Army Form C. 2118

Place	Date	Hour	Summary of Events and Information	Remarks and references to Appendices
NOEUX-LES-MINES	1.3.16		Inspection (funeral) of MAZINGARBE - PHILOSOPHE area. Satisfactory except for blocks of huts LE BRULOT FARM road occupied by fractured into 1 anchor gun craters etc. Lichens note lighter than usual owing to severe weather. 3-8. No infectious disease.	
"	2.3.16		Pumps used in two billet yards were found waterlogged. Construction went in entirety of incinerator completed. Weather - much milder. Roads + camp at muddy.	
"	3.3.16		Route section work. Inspected re Latrine area ARRAS Rd. municipal, crap 6 made to notify municipal Cie of D4L - 47 Pie. Saw Supervising Contractor works minute Precaution.	
"	4.3.16		Inspection of VERQUIN re case of Culicifugue. Colin re water of entrée etc. Disinfection of Billet at VERQUIN.	
"	5.3.16		Routine inspection. More cases hitchin re sanitation for Pl. Cpl. to Sad we are now attached Lecture reading.	
"	6.3.16		Interview with Sanitary Officer of 1st Div. Drawn re infantry June Francs inflict of Billet occupied by 10th Gordons. Stove chazgin from Rl. PHILOSOPHE - late notice treads of method for Endemic Latrine area. Sanitary Notice work - satisfactory. Schein note 4 - highest statement no infection	

WAR DIARY
or
INTELLIGENCE SUMMARY

(Erase heading not required.)

Army Form C. 2118

Instructions regarding War Diaries and Intelligence Summaries are contained in F. S. Regs., Part II. and the Staff Manual respectively. Title Pages will be prepared in manuscript.

Place	Date	Hour	Summary of Events and Information	Remarks and references to Appendices
NOEUX LES MINES	7/3/16		Routine work. Construction work in Catiro area in Area B' proceeding. Personnel Reinft. inspection in NOEUX-LES-MINES. Went with A.D.M.S. to various field ambulances. Sickness rate high – tonsilitis & chest trouble. Weather wet & cold.	JJ75
"	8/3/16		Went to MAZINGARBE & PHILOSOPHE. Rest infection — heavy shelling of PHILOSOPHE. Inspected satisfactory inspection of area round stone 3'.	JJ75
"	9/3/16		Analysis of 200S water supplies fairly satisfactory. Report sent in to A.D.M.S. Rest left today by 9' Black watch & 10' gordons. Routine work of inspection. Construction work at ARRAY R: area col. returns went at enbel. area. The damage had been caused by fire.	JJ75
"	10/3/16		General inspection & construction work. Trench supply maps completed for A.D.M.S.	JJ75
"	11/3/16		Completed general inspection of NOEUX water etc with Staff capt." then drew up & is doing with certain nuisances. Boards for water supplies altered & replaced. Routine work as usual.	JJ75

Army Form C. 2118

WAR DIARY
or
INTELLIGENCE SUMMARY
(Erase heading not required.)

Place	Date	Hour	Summary of Events and Information	Remarks and references to Appendices
NOEUX LES MINES	12/3/16		Section resting except for a few necessary inspections	
"	13/3/16		Routine inspecting by section. Completion of ventilation work in ARRAS no 1 area.	
"	14/3/16		Scheme drawn up & submitted for dealing with bad area outside rear HAUDRICOURT DROUVIN area. Routine inspection.	
"	15/3/16		Visited MAZINGARBE area. Interview with town major. PHILOSOPHE – See. Que interfered somewhat with inspection. Billets inspected round June 3. Also at cross roads. Pay parade at NOEUX LES MINES. Routine inspection work.	J/10
"	16/3/16		Conference re sanitary matters. DDMS, 1st Corps, 1st & 15th Division. General outline of work in line already adopted.	S/178
"	17/3/16		Inspection of NOEUX-LES-MINES area. Fatigue party for clearing old town dump (obtained by me) & fatigue party for dealing with manure in each area. Extension of work of 16th. Also purifying out water flooded billet yard. Visited LILLERS no 6 Co. & No 21 of Echelon NOEUX.	J/88
"	18/3/16		General inspection & extension of work of 17th. Interview with & letters to Town Major. NOEUX.	J/77.

WAR DIARY or INTELLIGENCE SUMMARY

Army Form C. 2118

(Erase heading not required.)

Place	Date	Hour	Summary of Events and Information	Remarks and references to Appendices
NOEUX LES MINES	19/3/16		Section resting except for supervision of necessary fatigue parties.	977B
"	20/3/16		Fatigue parties in ready of special manner. Life is expected of appx 70. Cleaning of old tram dug preserving. Peace inspection of rooms area in NOEUX LES MINES. General inspection work by section.	977B
"	21/3/16		Standards of O.C. 2nd Bn. 81. The will take over when we leave - to area & detailed orders of work. Inspected rooms area with him. Routine work by squads. Fatigue parties working at old dug & & rooms parts of the lines with two signs & cabins of rooms sanitary details.	977B
"	22/3/16		Partial school of neighbourhood with stephen & as with this was very limited cases of infectious disease known into the house. Health of town excellent. no actual infection shown except for cases of scale. Pointed out of section C.M.F. act 81 show area at VERQUIN. One slang of dust & various areas in the town. 87. Total no. men vaccinated was required by 2pe Sartz transport.	977B
"	23/3/16		Inspection of MAZINGARBE & VERQUIN PHILOSOPHE. Saw town majors of MAZINGARBE & Elect for acc'n 81. Water inspection. Collection of Religious & NOEUX	977B

WAR DIARY
or
INTELLIGENCE SUMMARY

Army Form C. 2118

(Erase heading not required.)

Place	Date	Hour	Summary of Events and Information	Remarks and references to Appendices
NOEUX LES MINES	24/3/16		Investigated infection with in NOEUX LES MINES - said to be produced by polluted water. Source infection probably Troops about moving back to LILLERS area early April. Suspect it easy to clean under TYPHOID & NOEUX.	Appx
"	25/3/16		Sent of stores out to Lillers. Sergt 81st sec' cured. Sergt 15th Div. Sect to LILLERS area & 16th Div of to NOEUX area. Inspection of water supplies and refuse.	Appx
			Inspected trenches of J. Garrison & 10th Gordons. Latrines & disposal systems.	Appx
			Back to the hole. Left after a good nothing.	Appx
"	26/3/16		Sergt 81st also went to NOEUX. at NOEUX MAZINGARBE returned to Bethune 3 pm.	
			Move to LILLERS & filled in new area.	
"	27/3/16		Infection work commenced all over area.	
LILLERS	28/3/16		Scheme of work drawn up.	
			Found out with ADMS to AMES re latrine epidemic	Appx
			to AMETTE re bathing facilities.	
"	29/3/16		Arranged lecture for M.O. & S.D. new army Div - renew Routine infection work. Went round area occupied by "Pantry" battalion ADMS Arranged for army for delivery water & "Pantry" Battalion. Complete sound inspection of LILLERS. Sources all from mayor	Appx

Army Form C. 2118

WAR DIARY
or
INTELLIGENCE SUMMARY

(Erase heading not required.)

Place	Date	Hour	Summary of Events and Information	Remarks and references to Appendices
LILLERS	30/3/16		Note: Instructions sent to troops with "Infection cases" lecture on Sanitation to officers. Ambulance & coln re Slaughter house annexe at RAINBERT.	378
"	31/3/16		Lecture at ALLOUAGNE O to whole duty men of 44th Brigade & Gunners. ② Sanitary Inspection of infection diseases to LILLERS. Disinfection of home which scarlet fever had been. Note: inspection	1779

Army Form C. 2118

WAR DIARY
or
INTELLIGENCE SUMMARY
(Erase heading not required.)

32 San Sec   Vol 9

SANITARY SECTION 32

Attached 15th Div.

APRIL 1916.

CONFIDENTIAL DIARY

J.H.Hawkes Capt. RAMC
OC San Sec 32

WAR DIARY
or
INTELLIGENCE SUMMARY

Army Form C. 2118

Place	Date	Hour	Summary of Events and Information	Remarks and references to Appendices
LILLERS	1/4/16		Investigated two cases of diphtheria. 6th Corps sent to C. Isl. Special hospital. Routine inspection work. Inspection of clothing depot. Lecture at AVEMEL to 46" Brigade at (1) on volunteer (2) Sanitation - also demonstration. Mumps & scabies. @ cholera (cavalry) @ Latrines LAPUGNOY	JJRS
"	2/4/16		General work - Lectures nothing.	
"	3/4/16		Lectures & demonstration at LAPUGNOY to 45" Brigade as (1) on Sanitation @ Sanitation hour 1 of each Battalion sent. Visits to field stations at LA BUISSIÈRE. Special sanitary work. Interview with DDMS re chief final latrines. Duty Batt: motor placed in arm at LOZINGHEM. Sets & demonstration to water duty men of 9" Gordons & A.S.C. 6" ALLOUAGNE re mumps (2 cases of dysentery) Cho 6 cases refused by 16" Div artillery attached to us.	JJRS
"	4/4/16		Guard routine work.	JJRS
"	5/4/16		Pay Parade. Inspection. Later for action during diurnal work.	JJRS

Place	Date	Hour	Summary of Events and Information	Remarks and references to Appendices
LILLIERS	6/4/16		General routine work. Unit Squad for units for divinal. Inner wheel consisting of various Flue squads marching with field ambces. Squad racing at LILLIERS. Investigate of cases of measles. S.F. at Lof LAPUGNOY camp + troops. Nyhnt & incinerary action.	JHS
"	7/4/16		1st day of divisional exercises. Section split up.	JHS
"	8/4/16		General routine work at LILLIERS. Squad in divisional exercises.	JHS
"	9/4/16		Return from divisional exercises.	JHS
"	10/4/16		General inspection work resumed. Inspection of advance, heaving state for old clothing. Informal talk with regard to dep Tunal Cture at 14oC. A.S.C. Disinfection of premises to be taken over by Mobility Sec. Cooker at reqnt of O.i.C.	JHS

WAR DIARY or INTELLIGENCE SUMMARY

Army Form C. 2118

Place	Date	Hour	Summary of Events and Information	Remarks and references to Appendices
LILLERS	11.4.16		Estimate of disinfection of premises of refugees contain hundreds - 1 disinfector - generators - Gas at NAIMBERT. Also gas at H.Q. Inspection at clothing depot. Routine work of section.	APP
"	12.4.16		Attempts re disinfected latrines in LILLERS area shew great difficulty owing to height of ground water & crumbling nature of subsoil. Stand until I place topped at 3½'. Advice given - clothing deflea special - Inoc a daily routine.	APP
"	13.4.16		Proceedin. General routine work & special inspection of HURIONVILLE area.	APP
"	14.4.16		Inspect of town began to provide latrines etc at YMCA hut. Special arrangts to BURBURE re 9th Nyd. Hyshr. Routine infection all over area.	APP

Army Form C. 2118.

WAR DIARY
or
INTELLIGENCE SUMMARY

(Erase heading not required.)

Instructions regarding War Diaries and Intelligence Summaries are contained in F. S. Regs., Part II. and the Staff Manual respectively. Title pages will be prepared in manuscript.

Hour, Date, Place	Summary of Events and Information	Remarks and references to Appendices
LILLERS. 15/4/16	Batt. fuel lecture in Corps political scheme*. Billet & YMCA hut. General routine work. All reports satisfactory.	JHB
" 16/4/16	Section voting.	JHB
" 17/4/16	Nothing special to report. General routine work. General health of Battalion excellent.	JHB
" 18/4/16	Parade of Section & lecture by C.O. re precautions to be taken during fly breeding season. Arrang's for destruction of material for cock etc. for nuisance etc. Experiment with deep trench latrines. Routine inspection, report satisfactory to old standards. Fm. may be covered a day too soon in circs. Locket to be had according to Corps indent. Sikhs admitted to C. Dnr. the use of J.P.B. men in reserve area.	JHB
" 19/4/16	Routine work. Guests. Pmd. inspection of Battalion. Billeted at ALLOUAGNE; headlights & aircraft at ALLOUAGNE — made refunct.	JHB

WAR DIARY
or
INTELLIGENCE SUMMARY
(Erase heading not required.)

Army Form C. 2118.

Hour, Date, Place	Summary of Events and Information	Remarks and references to Appendices
LILLERS 20/4/16	Introduction of S.C. San. Lec 22. Who takes over our hut next to Sanitary work, baths etc & neighbourhood. Special inspection & report upon TYPHOID at AMES. Routine work of inspection etc & y sectn. Investigation of case of P.U.O. at BURBURE - 9v. Blood taken. Report. Special inspection of RAIMBERT. General inspection work. Nothing special to report	JHD
LILLERS 21/4/16		JHD
LILLERS 22/4/16	General infection work. Scheme for new area formulated to A.D.M.S. Re-inoculation of half the section with T.A.B. Remainder to be done later.	JHD
LILLERS 23/4/16	Section resting. Investigation of cholera typhoid at AMETTES and FERFAY (one at FERFAY two & washing for me of the cases at AMES)	JHD
24/4/16	Troops start move into forward area. Lectures given to infection work & reporting on condition of civil billets etc as we left. Special inspection of clothing depot	JHD

WAR DIARY
or
INTELLIGENCE SUMMARY

(Erase heading not required.)

Army Form C. 2118.

Hour, Date, Place	Summary of Events and Information	Remarks and references to Appendices
LILLERS 25/4/16.	Inspection & report of new area left by the troops of 1st division. Small fatigue took rate over to SAILLY LA BOURSE with Serg. INCHLEY to go over new area & get in touch with any special work.	JFB
26/4/16	Part of morning stores re-filled, also two members of section in charge. Continuation of area inspection. Had scot over the area 23 to replace our own. T.W. new firm 12? drawn. Took over billets.	JFB
SAILLY "27/4/16.	Section moved from LILLERS to SAILLY took over billets left by 23 Sanitary Sech. Started to perform sanitation of new area	JFB
" 28/4/16	Finished sanitary duties at H.Q. found many defects, arrangements made to remedy these. General inspections being made all over area.	JFB

WAR DIARY
or
INTELLIGENCE SUMMARY

(Erase heading not required.)

Army Form C. 2118.

Hour, Date, Place	Summary of Events and Information	Remarks and references to Appendices
SAILLY. 29/4/16	General inspection work over whole area. Scavenging carts from #1, #2, 2 P.B. men. Parade inspection of JAVELLE, Timber Yard, Turkish but to NOEULLES & VERMELLES & on the sanitary condition at the Château. Damage again very defective plans, cellars much around & official suggested to adjutant refuse felling returned. Commanding officer visited Château — also has control of 15" (commanding officer) — the lorry sent to expo railhead at B.S.O. to see it. Ten loaded over 10 yds.	HHS
30/4/16	Drew Carbolic. Sect. notifyed of certain block rented to be permit inspection of centre instable.	HH

Army Form C. 2118.

32 Sen tr
Vol 10

WAR DIARY
or
INTELLIGENCE SUMMARY
(Erase heading not required.)

CONFIDENTIAL WAR
DIARY

San Sec 32 att 15th Division

May 1916.

J.F.Hawkes
Capt. D.a.C.D
O.C. San Sec. 32

COMMITTEE FOR THE
MEDICAL HISTORY OF THE WAR
Date 26 JUN 1915

WAR DIARY
or
INTELLIGENCE SUMMARY

(Erase heading not required.)

Army Form C. 2118.

Instructions regarding War Diaries and Intelligence Summaries are contained in F. S. Regs., Part II. and the Staff Manual respectively. Title pages will be prepared in manuscript.

Hour, Date, Place	Summary of Events and Information	Remarks and references to Appendices
SAILLY 1.5.16	Special inspection of Headquarters Col. NOELLES. Inspectory enlisting to be enlisted. Section carrying out work on new scheme found infections serving calls admitted & opened. Interview with Senior Officer of POIRIER. Good progress being made.	Appendix A & D. " 73
" 2.5.16	Inspection of POIRIER. Will pay my return. (Shells (up). Inspection of LA BOURSE. Very little work to be done. New system (Shells (N°1). Interview with medical officers. C.O°etc & the two relays. Great interest into the new area. Inspected one of Infant ought C° N°femme.	Appendix
" 3.5.16	Special inspection of RERUIGNEUIL. Progress being made. Saw new Calva. Interview with two officers re scheme for decly. Lieuves will continue before gates taken, interview with MAIRUS of wounded town. Found work progressing well.	

1247 W. 3299 200,000 (E) 8/14 J.P.C. & A. Forms/C. 2118/1.

Army Form C. 2118.

WAR DIARY
or
INTELLIGENCE SUMMARY

(Erase heading not required.)

Instructions regarding War Diaries and Intelligence Summaries are contained in F. S. Regs., Part II. and the Staff Manual respectively. Title pages will be prepared in manuscript.

Hour, Date, Place	Summary of Events and Information	Remarks and references to Appendices
SAILLY 4.5.16	Special report of ANNEQUIN sentry took VERMELLES pickel before dawn. Noticed good progress by 2 Offs Hagan (Calais) five P.B. an own B.C. & 46 Field ambulance, Elements Ry. Const. went with C.O. Litton	See attack C. 1975
5.5.16	Special inspection of FOUQUIÈRES & FOUQUEREUIL work progressing well especially will ASC units. Inspect Mis large dieset — BETHUNE call Refuse unusual scheme Command.	1975
6.5.16	Special inspects at H.Q. must informed at LABOURSE — the work is modifying E.O. of the whole of their ability to clear the so the Engineers	1975
7.5.16	Section until	1975

Army Form C. 2118.

WAR DIARY
or
INTELLIGENCE SUMMARY
(Erase heading not required.)

Instructions regarding War Diaries and Intelligence Summaries are contained in F. S. Regs., Part II. and the Staff Manual respectively. Title pages will be prepared in manuscript.

Hour, Date, Place	Summary of Events and Information	Remarks and references to Appendices
SAILLY 8.5.16.	Experiment finished with C solution. Septic infection of SAILLY sanitary very [?] today. Orders rec[?] today will sleep put latrine in 1st Life billets. Funny well is completed in SAILLY. Refuse collection scheme in free way.	
" 9.5.16	Stand ADMS. see notes. Arrangement in RERQUINGNEUIL [?] Forms D.A.E's along good work with ADMS & DADMS. Shower at SAILLY. Sector routine inspection. Gen'l work making good progress. Lt Col Fullerton elected a/s to C in BETHUNE. Commerce started [?] water [?] duties of looking two 70 new water supply at CLARKs Keep VERMELLES. Often water supply at NOYELLES with DADMS.	[signed]
" 10.5.16	Special inspection of NOYELLES with DADMS. 4 gardens along excellent work. Shower what for LAROUSSE Railway crossing. Bath etc Good progress made but less advanced than SAILLY.	[signed]

WAR DIARY
or
INTELLIGENCE SUMMARY
(Erase heading not required.)

Army Form C. 2118.

Hour, Date, Place	Summary of Events and Information	Remarks and references to Appendices
SAILLY 11.5.16	Special inspection of VERMELLES & ANNEQUIN with Sa Bde Comdr. Hoped to inspect trenches today but shelling to That Place on the out of shelling but Return in cool subjected. Two days but Return in cool Place Orders made 19 the action Lecture on Sanitation at School of Instruction between S O of BETHUNE GOSNAY. Pointed out various sanitary defects & issued instructions on chains — promise to rectify occupied by O. L.C. Turner Col att & luring VERMELLES trenches. He rode in the recti duties at CLARKES KEEP 2 T C men	MW
12.5.16	Cut down fir boy parade today. Extracts forward to CC Col Hopers cmd R.L. & Col wealta - 20 Col Lunday Monte unit preudy well.	MW

1247 W 3299 200,000 (E) 8/14 J.R.C. & A. Forms/C. 2118/11.

WAR DIARY
or
INTELLIGENCE SUMMARY

(Erase heading not required.)

Army Form C. 2118.

Hour, Date, Place	Summary of Events and Information	Remarks and references to Appendices
SAILLY LA BOURSE 13.5.16	Special inspection with DADMS of FOUQUIERES BETHUNE district. Inspect of Brigade H.Q. is upheld.	[illegible signature]
14.5.16	Minor - Cannot go day not eta Preliminary report from C.O. obtain Weather cold - much rain. Section roving.	[illegible]
15.5.16	Report in afternoon with Col admitted to A & one Cold much rain. Visits into CAMBRIN Fatigue parties for CUINCHY, LABOURSE, VERQUINEUIL, SAILLY [illegible] Schapely. Handed unit CRE re various details of hand sanitary work.	[illegible]
16.5.16	Special inspection SAILLY. Gas sanitary detail. Air fogging will. Day hot. Latrines hastily afflat. Seeing of scheme in fog. working as well. Work of NOEUX-LES-MINES much hoped of rapid.	[illegible]
17.5.16	Movement of troops. NOEUX-LES-MINES. Request for special fatigue party. Disinfector placed. JNM. three week need a translate.	[illegible]

WAR DIARY or INTELLIGENCE SUMMARY

Army Form C. 2118.

Hour, Date, Place	Summary of Events and Information	Remarks and references to Appendices
SAILLY. 18/5/16.	Special fatigue party commenced work at NOVELLES. Good progress. Shared inspected ANNEQUIN, VERMELLES. Shared inspected [illegible] at final. Reported arrival to ADMS in final. Disinfector 46 Divn collected and continued making excellent progress. Routine work.	Appendix E. JFB
" 19/5/16.	Special inspection of NOVELLES this day put between hay contractor etc + large amounts of the latter are flour reflected with cement. Cattle chimneys not [illegible] whatever making hay from. Further chimneys not [illegible] just like y of 1/10 vaults are extremely [illegible] x [illegible] as disinfect + unusual [illegible] effect quickly [illegible] [illegible]	JFB
" 20/5/16.	Special inspection BETHUNE + district. Routine work. Further chimneys with C Section - great difficulty in storing further supplies. Fatigue party carrying work at NOVELLES. Special report in final water supplies.	JFB

WAR DIARY or INTELLIGENCE SUMMARY

Army Form C. 2118.

Hour, Date, Place	Summary of Events and Information	Remarks and references to Appendices
SAILLY. 21/5/16	Section resting	
" 22/5/16	Further experiments with "C" oil. Revise fatigue party working in VERMELLES. N°One. 2 not report in C. not completed. 8 Doms Cyls (+) drawn from inspection. Special ingredient of older mixture Gustav. Good Showing. Investigation by trench projector of quel of distance getting to trench. Hints in Cuban Section observed - No ones observed in front of ave. Experiments with new type of C. oil getting by short range with little or no good for ships. Lodes Grey interior troubles. Special work at VERMELLES, NOYELLES.	J.H.B.
" 23/5/16	N° of SAILLY, LA BOURSE. Routine inspection work	J.H.B.

WAR DIARY
or
INTELLIGENCE SUMMARY

(Erase heading not required.)

Army Form C. 2118

Place	Date	Hour	Summary of Events and Information	Remarks and references to Appendices
SAILLY	24/5/16		Special went to NOYELLES, BETHUNE and Magnac BETHUNE. Suggested improvements & Wlletsburg Connect. out. 3 P.A. men charged	JHD
"	25/5/16		Shand went LABOURSE with 5 b of other ranks for entire return at VERMELLES. Lecture & contain to officer at School of Instruction. Section and order. Heavy clones and S.W.	JHD
"	26/6/.		Visit LABOURSE VERQUINEUL PERQUIN (received report from O.C. Train) route work. Pay parade. Recruit admitted up quota. Veletter & men Iro & book farmery Special inspection BETHUNE + FOUQUIÈRE District also artillery comp and VERQUINEUL. Routine section inspection	JHD
"	27/5/16		Inspection at HQ of 5. Div. Secln redng	JHD
"	28/5/16			JHD
"	29/5/16		Annual military & athletic - not interfering with the work. Shand went NOYELLES VERMELLES (2 Tommy attacks) deelng with Scontates (of the place) Interne with C.R.E. Route work	JHD

Army Form C. 2118

WAR DIARY
or
INTELLIGENCE SUMMARY
(Erase heading not required.)

Instructions regarding War Diaries and Intelligence Summaries are contained in F. S. Regs., Part II. and the Staff Manual respectively. Title Pages will be prepared in manuscript.

Place	Date	Hour	Summary of Events and Information	Remarks and references to Appendices
SAILLY	30/9.16		General inspection SAILLY. Instruction with a view to drainage improvement. Ruchs drawn for new revement. Photographic progress. Speed template of certain water supplies in LARWAIS	JPS JPD
"	31/9.16		General inspection NOYELLES. Routine work CEE over area. Summary of sundry incidents etc. in div. area. Appdx D	

WAR DIARY
or
INTELLIGENCE SUMMARY

(Erase heading not required.)

Army Form C. 2118.

Hour, Date, Place	Summary of Events and Information	Remarks and references to Appendices
SAILLY LA BOURSE	Scheme for fly bidy man — ① dustpits — 8-10ft with covers and hinged flaps Latrines — see estimate to be flyproof ② Buckets — boxed in (use netted punts?) Animals — to be as small as possible Drains placed & freed in life with proper funnel trap (see Du Kelley) Refuse Depots to cover note + for eulvage of me + mulch loss (1 — also to be delt with for destruction of impurties etc Du Velten + staff Sergt) Infection above tentaple O C Water Duty Sa + Cpl FITZGERALD Special fly mentagle Sea Cpl WRIGLEY. Trenches — Lce Cpl TOWNEND — BETHUNE — Lce CHEETANBRIDGE VERMELLES + PHILOSOPHE — MAXWELL — FOUQUEREIL — Lce GRAHAM Serg + BLENCH — FOUQUIERES — INCHLEY HOLT EMMETT BUNNER NOYELLES — TOPPING ANNEQUIN — O'CONNOR — Staffserg — Workshop etc — Lce Sergt BIRNIE SAILLY — BRODIE — Office — Pt PRIOR — Pt IVES (batmen) „ (& H.Q) — HARDY — Store etc — L Serg + JONES — PLUM LABOURSE — COLLINS — RUEDER (orderly) VERQUINEUIL — L Cpl LEATHER (dub band) — BRAINERD (Cook)	

J. F. Franks

WAR DIARY
or
INTELLIGENCE SUMMARY
(Erase heading not required.)

Army Form C. 2118.

Hour, Date, Place	Summary of Events and Information	Remarks and references to Appendices
	APPENDIX B	

Defence scheme

Two coys (X+Y) drawn etc from reserve bn. S.P. B---
from divisional coy any
Nylon shafts at LABOURSE (opposite huts). NOYELLES.
All oyer allocated for roads
Culverts notified & oyer placed outside in two etc
Two etc allocated for mountain areas

Int Tele   C. Coats
"a" out
ANNEQUIN   Present Thursday (morning)

LABOURSE   Monday & Thursday
                            Tuesday & Wednesday
NOYELLES   Wed - Saturday

SAILLY

VERQUINEUIL Tuesday, Friday

The few cook class mounted ares etc

All were carefully informed & checked up to date

WAR DIARY
or
INTELLIGENCE SUMMARY

Army Form C. 2118

APPENDIX C

Preliminary report on experiments carried out with "C" solution

For the first three days weather conditions were favourable to flies, being fine and warm; subsequently there changed to cold and windy with some rain.

Heap I. Refuse heap "A" — placed in drawer bench exposed to sunlight. Constituents — Human excreta, horse manure, food and other refuse. Dimensions 3' × 2' × 1'.

Refuse heap "B" — placed in a different kind of drawer bench under similar conditions and of identical composition. Was sprayed with 1 quart of "C" Solution after Pvt Loms "A" was sprayed with 1 quart of the heap in large numbers. The flies which had invaded the heap in large numbers died or flew away and the refuse was completely deodorized 4.5.16.

On May 7th the heap was still free from smell and no flies were observed.

Control heap "B" was covered with flies and had been constantly worked by them from the

WAR DIARY
or
INTELLIGENCE SUMMARY

Army Form C. 2118

Place	Date	Hour	Summary of Events and Information	Remarks and references to Appendices
			Time it was deposited (A rough fly trap had been placed over each heap after the treatment of (A) both the 4th inst. Trap "A" had no flies on it. Trap "B" contained many.)	
			On May 8th "A" still smelt fresh, but a few flies were lying on it. This more numerous	
	May 9th &10th			
	May 11th		Blow fly observed to deposit eggs on some meat lying on the surface of the treated heap. (These eggs had not hatched out 72 hours later.) Trap 2. A similar experiment to 1 was commenced on May 9th at 9 a.m. using half the quantity of "C" solution.	
	10/5/16		No smell. No flies	
	11/5/16		Several flies invaded heap. Trap 3 Decomposing sheeps heads — smelling badly. Almost covered with flies Sprayed lightly with "C" solution Observed later in the day — complete absence of smell. Flies dead. No sign of life, maggots or otherwise. (Unfortunately further observation was prevented as the head was removed.)	

WAR DIARY or INTELLIGENCE SUMMARY

Army Form C. 2118

(Erase heading not required.)

Place	Date	Hour	Summary of Events and Information	Remarks and references to Appendices

Feb 4. Ablution hut — floor made of tins which are full of time permeated with foul smelling soapy water etc. The smell was very bad, after the tins had been dug up in order to remove the floor, surface was sprayed with 'C' solution when seemed to act as a complete deodorant and the effect was lasting.

Feb 5. Two open latrine pails full of human excreta sprayed lightly with 'C' solution (The contents not treated but contents have upon which they stood also sprayed). Frequent observations made for 48 hours, but no flies were observed and the contents seemed to be completely deodorised. The experiments were interfered with by unfavourable weather conditions but seem to indicate that 'C' solution is effective as a deodorant and of great value as an antimiasma. The effects last for a considerable time but probably the application should be renewed after rain or after an interval of 48 hours. A Vermorel sprayer has been used in all experiments. The solution seems to have a harmful effect upon the rubber washers.

WAR DIARY
or
INTELLIGENCE SUMMARY

Army Form C. 2118

2nd Report on "C" Solution (used in various Kengkos)

Weather conditions – Hot

(1) Pun pit (about 36 sq feet) containing two heaps of refuse (manure, meat, cheese, human excreta) and some decomposed meat. Much smell, innumerable flies.

17.5.1916. 9.30 a.m. Sprayed freely with 5% C. Solution (about 4 galls used for whole pun pit)

+ p.m. Smell and flies much reduced.

18.5.1916. Considerable smell. Flies increasing

19.5.1916. Smell very bad. Flies numerous.
Sprayed freely with 'C' Solution 10%

20.5.1916. Smell reduced but still evident.
6 p.m. Heaps sprayed with 20% solution

21.5.1916. No smell. No flies.

22.5.1916. Smell perceptible. Few flies.

(2) Two faeces

WAR DIARY
or
INTELLIGENCE SUMMARY
(Erase heading not required.)

Army Form C. 2118

Place	Date	Hour	Summary of Events and Information	Remarks and references to Appendices
			(2) Two pieces of horse flesh placed on a bench 16.5.1916	
			A)	
			17.5.1916. Surface sprayed freely with 'C' Solution 5%.	17.5.1916. Untreated. Many flies
			18.5.1916. Surface "leathery" visited by one or two flies.	18.5.1916. Covered with flies (blue bottles, green bottles etc) Many eggs
			19.5.1916. A few more flies & some slushes of eggs on surface. No smell	19.5.1916. Much smell. Many larvae
			20.5.1916. No smell. Larvae in cracks which were not treated	20.5.1916. Advanced composition much smell. Milling of larvae. Sprayed 20% 'C' Solution. Completely deodorised. Maggots dead
			21.5.16 } Many larvae 22.5.16 } Slight smell	21.5.16 Very little smell all flies no flies
			(3) Dead dog (about 4 to 5) in advanced stage of decomposition. Much smell. Covered with flies.	
			21.5.16. Sprayed with 20% solution. Deodorised	This killed completely
			22.5.16 (24 hrs later) Still no smell but flies returning	

WAR DIARY
or
INTELLIGENCE SUMMARY

(Erase heading not required.)

Army Form C. 2118

Place	Date	Hour	Summary of Events and Information	Remarks and references to Appendices
			(4) Experiment with maggots. Piece of meat "alive with" larvae.	
		10.30 am	Sprayed with 20% hy kitty.	
		11.30 am	majority dead	
		4.30 pm	all maggots dead	
			(5% seems to drive the maggots into the centre but has not sufficient power to exterminate them completely)	
			(5) Burned heap sprayed with undilute "C" solution 4/5/16	
			No smell. No eggs for 1 day.	
		19.5.1916.	maggots appeared and in places the heap was noticed to be swelling	
		20.5.1916.	many maggots	
			Sprayed lightly with 10% when killed the maggots and deodorised	
			(The lasting effect of pure "C" solution was very noticeable in this experiment.)	
			(6) Foul smelling yard to filler (Pig sty, soapy water, old refuses)	
		17.5.16	Sprayed free 5% "C" solution. 4½ gallons used.	
			Deodorised completely.	
		18.5.16	Much improved.	
		19.5.16	Smell returning	

WAR DIARY or INTELLIGENCE SUMMARY

Army Form C. 2118

(1) Manure heap (pig horse dung) had smell covered with flies and full of maggots. Sprayed fully with 5% 'C' solution. Flies killed, smell abolished — for a few hours only, maggots driven into centre of heap. No dead ones found. Men in the trenches. Reports state that foul smelling "dug outs" are quickly made habitable by spraying with "C" solution 5%.

Latrine Buckets. These and small much stained by spraying with 5% 'C' Solution. The smell from lightly sprinkling the skin and platform with and whilst 'C' solution is excellent.

Comment. In my opinion 'C' solution should be used in full strength when treating carcases etc. 10-20% strength for spraying refuse which cannot be dealt with otherwise: a 5% strength for "dugouts", "latrines" dealt with otherwise. "cookhouses" etc.

A rough watering can for using the solution may be made with a few minutes from a 4 gallon non-returnable petrol tin.

Remarks and references to Appendices

Army Form C. 2118.

WAR DIARY
or
INTELLIGENCE SUMMARY.
(Erase heading not required.)

Instructions regarding War Diaries and Intelligence Summaries are contained in F. S. Regs., Part II. and the Staff Manual respectively. Title pages will be prepared in manuscript.

Hour, Date, Place	Summary of Events and Information	Remarks and references to Appendices
	Holes should be made as provided. The outside turn-ins are fully; they should be bored in the lid helpful and close to the edge most remote from the stopper and should not be nearer together than 3/4". Two rows are required above as shewn. This has been used in the [?]	

(73989) W.4141—463. 400,000. 9/14. H.&J.Ltd. Forms/C. 2118/10.

WAR DIARY
or
INTELLIGENCE SUMMARY

(Erase heading not required.)

Army Form C. 2118

Place	Date	Hour	Summary of Events and Information	Remarks and references to Appendices
Alluoli	D		Summary of latrines etc "155" div cec	
			Deep pit latrines - Cupfully covered type 65 }	
			Pail latrines " 24 }	
			" " not covered 21 }	
			Accumulators - 5.62 sets.	
			Urinals (Reeed + type + trough a funnel) 92	
			Incinerators in daily use (ram type) 67	
			Ablution benches 25	
			heat 3cfm 19	

WAR DIARY
or
INTELLIGENCE SUMMARY
(Erase heading not required.)

Army Form C. 2118

Appendix E
Trench Sanitation Summary of what the Inspector of Sownes

In view of the approach of hot weather with the inevitable resultant trails of rapid decomposition, and smells, immense thus trench sanitation becomes a nuisance importance when though secondary to military considerations (makes it rank as in essentials in any scheme where it serves to military in trench warfare it is quite impossible to clear it as a side issue to be dealt with when circumstances permit, but.

The following notes extracted from the various reports of the sanitary inspector in charge of trench work are wholly of construction. The persons engaged in these reports say they are of immediate military activity and it is possible that some of the statements could be modified under more favourable circumstances.

Deep pits with fly proof covers for use as latrines, there can be no doubt that where these are able to be constructed they will:-

① decrease the fly nuisance & reduce risk of fly born infection
② involve less onerous work for the sanitary duty men

WAR DIARY
or
INTELLIGENCE SUMMARY
(Erase heading not required.)

Army Form C. 2118

Instructions regarding War Diaries and Intelligence Summaries are contained in F.S. Regs., Part II and the Staff Manual respectively. Title Pages will be prepared in manuscript.

Place	Date	Hour	Summary of Events and Information	Remarks and references to Appendices
			(3) Involve two men for the sanitary duty men be drawn and per arrival. The alternative system of "pals" and burying the contents has certain obvious objections. (A) Careless men notify tip the contents over the parapet (B) Careful men crawl on and bury the contents in a shell hole of some upon the danger, but it is seen that on Battalion has for sanitary men whilst engaged on this work often state that for various reasons there is little danger and the work can be properly done. (C.) In no case is such a procedure capable of careful supervision. For certain positions the excreta can be buried in the floor of an disused sap. [A.B. + C.] Criticisms on Deep Pits. (1) Much primary work is involved the result is exposed positions is liable at any moment to be obliterated with consequent disorganisation until further work can be undertaken. (2) The work when carried on in the front or support line is liable to be observed by the enemy who may effect a machine gun emplacement and accordingly. (3) In certain places water is reached before the pit is of sufficient depth.	

1875 Wt. W593/826 1,000,000 4/15 J.B.C. & A. A.D.S.S./Forms/C. 2118.

Army Form C. 2118

WAR DIARY
or
INTELLIGENCE SUMMARY
(Erase heading not required.)

Instructions regarding War Diaries and Intelligence Summaries are contained in F. S. Regs., Part II. and the Staff Manual respectively. Title Pages will be prepared in manuscript.

Place	Date	Hour	Summary of Events and Information	Remarks and references to Appendices
			(4) To be of value these pits must be of a considerable depth. There is a natural tendency to dig them too shallow and where sufficient depth is attained there is a tendency for the sides to fall in during wet weather or when there is heavy shelling. Comments. 1 and 3 are not objections to the system in the front support trenches by dealing with the & earlier. Probably 2 could be overcome by training the men in it are of real importance, but need further mature in the nearer manner. The points raised in 4 are of real importance, but need further evidence. The nearer officer in experience of many states emphatically that it is impossible to dig a pit of the required depth dimensions without specially trained officers against the whole the opinions of medical officers is in favour of these deep pits in the front support, but is in this reserve. Communication trenches of them for the reserve. They should certainly be provided with some form of cover; tiny corrugated iron bent true their heads have to be used, they should certainly be also canvas covers coated with creosote both are useless probably some simple form of loose eat such a lid when not automatically to close wires need with the difficulty	

Army Form C. 2118

WAR DIARY
or
INTELLIGENCE SUMMARY

(Erase heading not required.)

Instructions regarding War Diaries and Intelligence Summaries are contained in F. S. Regs., Part II. and the Staff Manual respectively. Title Pages will be prepared in manuscript.

Place	Date	Hour	Summary of Events and Information	Remarks and references to Appendices

Some latrines are much used, others only occasionally & yet in no case is more than one bucket provided. Even in the case that erecta buckets are constantly overflowing and in new positions additional accommodation should be provided. The reports show that organically very little effort to keep latrines in a sanitary condition is made to Rup. Left for two or three days without attention, buckets fitting till the communication trenches run a river, also that in the someninication trenches is responsible for this neglect owing to doubt as to who is responsible for this work. This needs some regulation.

"C" Solution is proving of great value. When sponges (diluted 1 in 20) in deep dug outs it quickly abolishes unpleasant conditions and of use for the latrines so that etc. etc. is is deodorizing and abolishing the nuisance

Seats pierced by many above the vertical

WAR DIARY
or
INTELLIGENCE SUMMARY
(Erase heading not required.)

Army Form C. 2118

Instructions regarding War Diaries and Intelligence Summaries are contained in F.S. Regs., Part II. and the Staff Manual respectively. Title Pages will be prepared in manuscript.

Place	Date	Hour	Summary of Events and Information	Remarks and references to Appendices
			I would suggest that all latrines be sprayed twice daily with dilute "C" solution and where flies are bad that the urinals and surroundings be sprayed each morning with strong solution in addition.	J.P.Jack J/Cpt

Monthly sanitary report for June

T. Hewlett
Capt. R.A.M.C.
O.C. San...

Army Form C. 2118.

WAR DIARY
or
INTELLIGENCE SUMMARY

(Erase heading not required.)

CONFIDENTIAL WAR DIARY

San Sec 32. att'd 15th Div.

June 1916

J.H. Saunders
Capt. No on C (T)
O.C. San Sec 32

WAR DIARY
or
INTELLIGENCE SUMMARY

Army Form C. 2118

Place	Date	Hour	Summary of Events and Information	Remarks and references to Appendices
SAILLY	1.6.16		Routine inspection work. Spent of [morning] inspecting hutments for G.O.C. [?] Noyelles not taken over but [?] du [relief]. Visited APM re emply frame huts at NOEUX [Les Mines] OC 16 du [Railway] Co.	977b
	2.6.16		Visited NOEUX billets re total of empty [huts]. [?] refugees into nurses at LAROUSE. Sanitary reports copied & submitted to A.D.M.S. Routine work. Recents convened at LAROUSE (BETHUNE district).	977b 9/14
	3.6.16		Capt. Spence inspection of beds area (result 2) Saple of water from Tinches - (result 2) Routine work holding special to report.	977b 9/14
	4.6.16		Sections voting.	
	5.6.16		Sent report from action with regard to cubic medition. Spread inspection of LAROUSE - REQUIGNEUIL. P. OLIVER (h.e. alcohol) examined sick. Sands puf drown for engineer.	977b
	6.6.16		Spread inspection NOELLES with SADMS. Wetly and - [patg] hay stones. Sent out in ANNEQUIN + REQUIGNEUIL. Spread infection to all the parts of accomodation (sanitary) returned into an O.	977b
	7.6.16		Routine work. Remarks water construction in LAROUSE. Walter James Catting M.O.	977b

Army Form C. 2118

WAR DIARY
or
INTELLIGENCE SUMMARY
(Erase heading not required.)

Instructions regarding War Diaries and Intelligence Summaries are contained in F.S. Regs., Part II. and the Staff Manual respectively. Title Pages will be prepared in manuscript.

Place	Date	Hour	Summary of Events and Information	Remarks and references to Appendices
SAILLY	8/1/16		Three hours inspection of trenches - trench supplies - Coy bombers - dug outs Latrines etc. - Area expected for QUARRY ALLEY TO HILLOCK N.S. Inspection of FERMELLES. Pumping at billet yard in LABOURSE. Dentist work practice. 3rd Fd of work obtained from Engineers, also return supplied for contracts with work carried out made with 4 & 7 F.C. to carry ES before withdrawn. Little other news. New deep pit latrine (J. Retzlow way) in REQUIGNEUIL	J.773
"	9/1/16		Special inspection with A Div of divisional schools. ohm geometre Latrines etc. Two extra Latrines made Garden etc. Cultures for Latrine Pit yard continued. Pumping of yard continued. Dentists inspection. Pumps ponds etc.	J.773 J.774
"	10/1/16		Pumps at LABOURSE. Dentists inspection. Visit to NOYELLES at request of CO 9th Foot re refuse dumps.	J.774
"	11/1/16		Latrines nothing.	J.774

1875 W: W593/826 1,000,000 4/15 J.B.C. & A. A.D.S.S./Forms/C. 2118.

WAR DIARY
or
INTELLIGENCE SUMMARY

(Erase heading not required.)

Army Form C. 2118

Instructions regarding War Diaries and Intelligence Summaries are contained in F. S. Regs. Part II. and the Staff Manual respectively. Title Pages will be prepared in manuscript.

Place	Date	Hour	Summary of Events and Information	Remarks and references to Appendices
SAILLY	12/6/16		Special inspection VERQUIGNEUL LA BOURSE VENDIN. Inspections etc. Pumping at LA BOURSE of hitherto large reent 8ft in bad condition by 8 Reynolds, at LA BOURSE	JTTS
	13/4/16		Special inspection of SAILLY. Everything in excellent order. Visited Bde. Goren BETHUNE with A Dn. S. Putting work by hands. Janse undue into inspection	JTTS
	14/6/16		Special inspection NOEULLES. All satisfactory. Pumping work at LA BOURSE by fatigue party of prisoners. Cafield analysis of all repairs for 5 weeks	JTTS
	15/6/16		Special went to ANNEQUIN. Statutory connection commenced. Some trouble owing to civilian duty in officer. Allegation of refusal in incident - action in two LIAISON officer. Reported to AP re attitude of LA BOURSE re fatigue party of prisoners for LA BOURSE refuse dumps. Cease. Lecture by OC at Div School in sanitation. Weather continues "very wet" in d N.V.	JTTS

WAR DIARY
or
INTELLIGENCE SUMMARY
(Erase heading not required.)

Army Form C. 2118

Place	Date	Hour	Summary of Events and Information	Remarks and references to Appendices
SAILLY	14/6/16		Routine inspection work. Nothing special to report	
"	15/6/16		Heavy traffic to ANNEQUIN especially of 4" Bn attached for instruction. Special train to meet the extra demand for return to BETHUNE.	
			O.C. attached 2nd & 3rd Bns ct— Section voting except for men carried out at rifle range. LAROUSSE with Lt. D.C. of 4" Bn as firer for instruction.	
"	18/6/16		Visited VERMELLES, NOYELLES, VERQUIGNEUL, SAILLY, Bethune Rums. Went over officers papers etc.	
			Very cohere report from infantry at VERMELLES re known locations of VERMELLES. Sergt Blood asked to report. Sergt of Jery Bn returned with information attached for instruction.	
			Are very crowded owing to drawn LAROUSSE ejected from an enemy in no mans land (inf.try b) very close to enemy's trenches. Left trenches early to entrain rifle for training to establish into an officer.	
"	20/6/16		Visited VERQUIGNEUL re report of own put "Cauldry silor full of foul water"	

Army Form C. 2118

WAR DIARY
or
INTELLIGENCE SUMMARY
(Erase heading not required.)

Instructions regarding War Diaries and Intelligence Summaries are contained in F. S. Regs., Part II. and the Staff Manual respectively. Title Pages will be prepared in manuscript.

Place	Date	Hour	Summary of Events and Information	Remarks and references to Appendices
SAILLY	21/6/16		Lectures on the of not very bad fleas &c. Endured stine notified mud-covered & refused to tDnr Sgt. Shot refused report yh. VERMELLES sabre chain up & admitted to ADMS. Suggested upkeep will good to level of entch of babat also Lining of traces hundred of various were kept for fly breeding at plant, army to old weather.	PPS
"	22/6/16		Lectures in Sanitation at Div School. Several inspection of VERQUIGNEUL & LABOURSE. Drain work hufect of Houdain & SAILLY & Cafes commander hupectin of billets in LABOURSE & VERQUIGNEUL by Cnfs commander. Drains inspection work.	PS
"	23/6/16		Return visit AD PMO re roofs accompany a modern inspector BETHUNE area. The new roofing rate for Div than are very unsettled at the a little available ground.	PS
"	24/6/16		Drain work. Several latine contracts at VERMELLES with Petique hilly. @ Run 4.7 Fc.	PS

Army Form C. 2118

WAR DIARY
or
INTELLIGENCE SUMMARY
(Erase heading not required.)

Instructions regarding War Diaries and Intelligence Summaries are contained in F. S. Regs., Part II. and the Staff Manual respectively. Title Pages will be prepared in manuscript.

Place	Date	Hour	Summary of Events and Information	Remarks and references to Appendices
JAILLY	25/6/16		Section noting. Instructional work at VERMELLES continued.	
	26/6/16		Hrs VERMELLES sent to trenches. Arranged for P.O. men to look after new section trenches at LAROUVRE. Special inspection of VERQUINEUR — men on lab noticed — now working. Latrines made emptied at VERMELLES. Commenced work. Night working party for mine at VERMELLES.	JHJ
	27/4/16		Special inspection of sunken rockets to LAROUVRE. JAILLY at VERMELLES continued. Working party for mine at VERMELLES. VERQUINEUR. Visited rest of 2nd D.I. at regt of gardens & reported to ADMS.	JHJ
	28/4/16		Special inspection of NOVELLES. Fly infect sent to ADMS. Growth of burned oats for filthy retreats in LAROUVRE good. No house washing — not available for retreat. Careful inventory at LAROUVRE stated working. Working party at VERMELLES.	
	29/6/16		Inspection of waste drains round JAILLY. Special inspection LAROUVRE drains not functional. Advise upset for clothing etc.	JHJ

Army Form C. 2118

WAR DIARY
or
INTELLIGENCE SUMMARY
(Erase heading not required.)

Place	Date	Hour	Summary of Events and Information	Remarks and references to Appendices
PAILLY	29/6/16		Head went to BETHUNE re "Clothing store". Fatigue parties working on nameic dump at PAILLY & refuse dump & LABOURSE Douane refuse dump.	

Army Form C. 2118

WAR DIARY
or
INTELLIGENCE SUMMARY
(Erase heading not required.)

Vol 12

CONFIDENTIAL WAR DIARY

San Sec 32   Att'd 15th Div

July 1916.

COMMITTEE FOR THE
MEDICAL HISTORY OF THE WAR
Date 5 - SEP. 1916

J.H. Hawkins
Capt. R.A.M.C.
O.C. S. San Sec 32

Army Form C. 2118

WAR DIARY
or
INTELLIGENCE SUMMARY
(Erase heading not required.)

Instructions regarding War Diaries and Intelligence Summaries are contained in F.S. Regs., Part II. and the Staff Manual respectively. Title Pages will be prepared in manuscript.

Place	Date	Hour	Summary of Events and Information	Remarks and references to Appendices
SAILLY LA BOURSE	1/7/16		Shead went to BETHUNE. Took at the Wh. Tobacco factory & Orphanage - good condition transformed to a new cnf (3rd cnf in three weeks) then is getting into order but outfit never went upon the works. Thankful tim we still carry traffic by Grenadier estate tops etc. refunt out in. Have dist forced E of Clos del Pres, in Ditches with inches of mages. New transals at LABOURSE of working well.	JJ?
	2/7/16		Party went to E of Cuttmes completed fatigue party want to VERMELLES to split upon elevation.	JJ?
	3/7/16		Shead inspection LABOURSE VERQUINEUL (bttln not before - never over supply - refnt) Grft for us is two new men - very satisfactory. Parts int.	J/18
			Cleaning work at VERMELLES.	
	4/7/16		Shead went to VERMELLES — work finishing well. Very very rain — Thunderstorm in a.m.	J/18
	5/7/16		Parts ints. Nothing special to refnt.	J/18
	6/7/16		2nd Lieut Pte RICHARDS. E.T (3117) Nicholaetts arrived to replace 2. C. BUNKER.	J/?
			Shead inspect of cnfs in LABOURSE etc — names chifs REQUINENSE bring carrys & paunera. Parts inspections.	J/?

1875 Wt. W 593/826 1,000,000 4/15 J.B.C. & A. A.D.S.S./Forms/C. 2118.

WAR DIARY
or
INTELLIGENCE SUMMARY

(Erase heading not required.)

Army Form C. 2118

Place	Date	Hour	Summary of Events and Information	Remarks and references to Appendices
SAILLY	7/7/16		Special inspection with A.D.M.S. of billets in LABOURSE & VERQUIGNEUL. Owing to drains is very difficult owing to closure of sunken pipe drains. Pay parade 6 pm	
"	8/7/16		Fatigue party completed work at VERMELLES. Pioneers clearing refuse round LABOURSE dumps. Routine inspection took place. Went if road to Coal mine as feeling chasms collapse	
"	9/7/16		Section resting	
"	10/7/16		Special inspection at LABOURSE, SAILLY, VERQUIGNEUL, between L. boom office & tunnels all sunken sump pits, caves etc. Routine work	
"	11/7/16		Weather autumn cold & windy (W) very little fly trouble. Routine work as usual knees. Tile infection practice & ptin.	
"	12/7/16		Lecture delivered by O.C. on sanitation at Brunswick school (comme) friends unit of Divmen artillery corps	
"	13/7/16		Night work. Lecture to section in duties we drum is in to march.	

Army Form C. 2118

WAR DIARY
or
INTELLIGENCE SUMMARY
(Erase heading not required.)

Place	Date	Hour	Summary of Events and Information	Remarks and references to Appendices
SAILLY	14/7/16		Special visit to "NOYELLES". Road narrow, caused by mud & 8" Bn & Infantry occupation of some of the huts. 2 coure dugouts need further attention. Ponton Inspection. Special visit to billets at BETHUNE. Section – Joined women much in t N.W. side very little fly breeding. Routine Inspection work.	JFB
"	15/7/16		Special visit to BETHUNE re manure at exchange. (Flooded cellar) act to inspect Plogstn dysenteric station. Section acting.	JFB
"	16/7/16		NOYELLES. PHILOSOPHE. VERMELLES. Communication trenches.	JFB
"	17/7/16		Special inspection. Such yourself at VERMELLES & garden at PHILOSOPHE except. Inspected latrines of one of the Battns. Pioneers working in dug out at NOYELLES. The communication trenches still present difficulties, fatig for sanitary work too small: 5 ft 19½ unles.	JFB
"	18/7/16		Routine inspection work. Inspection of stores & required to do Eng Ord. Field Lab'y.	JFB
"	19/7/16		Pitting special to about. CCC areas in satisfactory cadd.	JFB

WAR DIARY
or
INTELLIGENCE SUMMARY

Army Form C. 2118

(Erase heading not required.)

Place	Date	Hour	Summary of Events and Information	Remarks and references to Appendices
SAILLY	29/7/16		Fine sunshine. Received clothing. Pyjamas & manure bags. A Dr & Section of F.E. men in sanitary work. Several cases of scarmine. Notes upon activities at large cattle leak at LAROUSE embarking men hurrying to return to cultivate their crops rather military in civilian dress other military in civilian.	
"	21/7/16		Payparade. Kent round area with sanitary officer taking over district. Attached early Preparations completed for moving. Section split up so that unit can be regularly inspected during move. Distribution:	

Sgt. RLENCH L/Cpl. BIRNIE 13" Royal Scots L/Sergt INGRAM 7/8 KOSB
L/Cpl. FITZGERALD 8. Seaforths   L/Cpl WRIGLEY 9/7 R.S.F. L/Cpl O'CONNOR 10/11 H.L.I.
" HOLT 9" Royal Highlanders   L/Cpl CM   " HARDY 12 H.L.I.
" MAXWELL 8/10 Gordons   " TOPPING   " BRODIE 10 Yorks.
" STANDRIDGE 7" Cameron   " EMMETT 11 A+S High.

GRAHAM Train   L/Cpl TOWNEND HQ

" COLLINS Lanfret R.F.A. Pt RICHARDS. HQ
" LEATHER D.A.C.   Spr GLOVER
                        A.S.C. Driver M.T. KINNEAR

S.S. HQ
Staff Sergt.
Sergt JONES Storeclk
Pte BRANNERD Cook
     ROEDER   Orderly
     PLUMB   Batman
     IVEN   Cotmyr.
     PRIOR   Clerk

WAR DIARY
or
INTELLIGENCE SUMMARY.
(Erase heading not required.)

Army Form C. 2118.

Place	Date	Hour	Summary of Events and Information	Remarks and references to Appendices
BRAY	22/9/16		Troops moving. S.S. will work. L/C. A.J. moved to BRYAN for	JWD
"	23/9/16		SALLY LA BOURSE arrived 3 p.m. Capt. Delabole & 4 pnrs in motor convoy. Sect. under Capt. Letot bivouac in field close & billet	JWD
"	24/9/16		Under 44 Brigade area. Party cook of L/Cpl. Cannon tak. reported to E.M.O. Returned. D/Sect. L/Cpl. Miller inspired Lt Fitzgerald S.P. Bureau	JWD
"			Orders to move on 26th.	
"	25/9/16		Entered area of 45" Brigade with A.D.M.S. Inspected Dyer's Sect + R.E.I. L/Cpl. Feather (motor driver) lent detached for work with M.O.	JWD
"			Interviewed L/Cpl. Kingley	
FLERS	26/9/16		Left BRAS 2 A.M. Arrived FLERS 11.00 A.M. Capped for night. Parties work by men with mules	JWD
FROHEN-LE-GRAND	27/9/16		Left FLERS 8 A.M. Arrived FROHEN-LE-GRAND 11 A.M. Sectn. under Cannon. Work with mules	JWD
BERNAVILLE	28/9/16		Left FROHEN-LE-GRAND 9 A.M. Arrived BERNAVILLE 12.30 P.M. Sectn. under Cannon. Work with mules	JWD

WAR DIARY
INTELLIGENCE SUMMARY

Army Form C. 2118.

Place	Date	Hour	Summary of Events and Information	Remarks and references to Appendices
BERNAVILLE	29/7/16		Visited seven huts of 4th & 44 Brigades. Sanitary arrangements working out excellently. All Medical officers ylad. Well of work done by its men detailed to look into unit in question. Under officers have great difficulty in getting the filth removed at all officers ur woe, about a sufficient water can be obtained testing water.	
"	30/7/16			
VIGNACOURT	31/7/16		Moved to VIGNACOURT. Found excellent digs, well caught out by owners unyholsky. Town myn had asked for water to be placed on their wells, as nothing had been done I too were pleased of action. I ordered me B. to write the matter to ur. D.M.S. Victor - Pie I a. To pective very high. Ecole Touidub	

T2134. W. W708—776. 500000. 4/15. Sir J.C. & S.

WAR DIARY
or
INTELLIGENCE SUMMARY.

Army Form C. 2118.

Summary of Events and Information

15 Aug.

CONFIDENTIAL WAR DIARY.

AUGUST 1916.

SANITARY SECTION 32 } 1 2nd Sanitary Co.
as 15th Div.

COMMITTEE FOR THE
MEDICAL HISTORY OF THE WAR
Date -5 OCT 1916

J.H. Sawkins.
Capt R.A.M.C.
O.C. S.S. 32.

Army Form C. 2118.

WAR DIARY
or
INTELLIGENCE SUMMARY.
(Erase heading not required.)

Place	Date	Hour	Summary of Events and Information	Remarks and references to Appendices
PIGNACOURT	1/8/16		Section split up amongst various units (as shown on diary for July) during chrome movements. Inter-infection supervision & advice. Gee medical officer then G.T. Army to the relief of the Scheme. Special visit to FLESSELLES. Known well and no of 7.T.H.L. Latter placed on well in MONACOURT as soldiers had to change washing effects. Heather fine & perfect but Douthe went amongst troops. Nothing special to report.	J.T.S.
"	2/8/16		" " " "	J.T.S.
"	3/8/16		" Visited 45 & 44 Depot	J.T.S.
St GRATIEN	4/8/16		Moved to St GRATIEN	J.A.
BAIZIEUX	5/8/16		Moved to BAIZIEUX. Known with sanitary officer of 1st Div. Went round of bathing bolton & water supplies. Douthe went amongst troops. Nothing special to report	J.T.S.
"	6/8/16		Visited ALBERT & sanitary one allotted to divan E. of ALBERT. Known in above division & sanitary officer of 33 Div. Discussion of sanitary scheme with N.O.s & TRAMWAY. Decided to recall to man horsemen	J.T.S.

WAR DIARY
or
INTELLIGENCE SUMMARY.
(Erase heading not required.)

Army Form C. 2118.

Place	Date	Hour	Summary of Events and Information	Remarks and references to Appendices
ALBERT	5/8/16		Section moved H.Q. to ALBERT [cap. in october]	
"	9/8/16		Issued recepts of our allotted & copies for boundary references on S.E. of ALBERT. Parties took 9 men with mules	
"	10/8/16		Inspection of ground around FRICOURT, CONTALMAISON & SHELTER WOOD for BIVVIE, IMPLET & G.D. HOLT. BRODIE, IMMET would make v. fine area work. Carried out 500 p. supply of fosses & squares for wood canvas, nails etc.	
"	11/8/16		Sergt BLENCH reported & att.chd cult L.C. HOLT & BRODIE to work and reconn'r area. Return for over fall again.	
"	12/8/16		Catriole of recent & estim for new Hdqrts. cap. Carry of old cap refined. Parties inspected work. Sick away & p. one of mules & 2 letters for inspection. TOPPING S.E.C--- OCONNOR 5/8 N.S.R. HARRY 12 HLI FITZGERALD 5.9 Suffolk WRIGLEY 5/4 R.C.F 9 Bluebords 12 N.A. Scots John HOLT	JSH JSH JSH JSH JSH

WAR DIARY

Army Form C. 2118.

Place	Date	Hour	Summary of Events and Information	Remarks and references to Appendices
Nr. ALBERT	13/8/16		Routine work. Captain of HQ work. Inspection of Transport Lines — Chiefly disgraceful. Have Con. has been in charge of this Coy for months.	
"	14/8/16		Capt. McHARDIE (?) the noted regular charge up tonight. Visited allotted area — went over trench well. Serg RENCH (orderly) returns. Two letters notified.	(770)
"	15/8/16		Visited reserve brigade area, see enough has been made but left 2nd Lt over tonight line, which returns. Head went to battalion area behind advanced to the train. Police topo, ads for all transport lines. Drew up full details of section to meet Coe's on return of our own infected the whole area. Coy afft admirable of scratch seems to have been chiefly futile; none is depended on new tactics. Return as nothing happened & there is no infirmity. Cafes are closed by 9:30 & will close after but please i moved.	(770)

WAR DIARY
or
INTELLIGENCE SUMMARY.
(Erase heading not required.)

Army Form C. 2118.

Place	Date	Hour	Summary of Events and Information	Remarks and references to Appendices
ALBERT	10/9/16		Visited informent camp. Sentry calling difficult hillside couldn't understand control. Op. & Pol. between class to each near etc. No sentry up by day. Colonel to visit ration & forward dumps & hull up 2nd line dumps at Ln & Oct - arrangement for 15 Corps down not are allotted to its own Divisional Reference to 15 Corps area at L. Corps battle refused to I.L.9. for & each latrine life & flattest fr. were dugouts are perlin moved.
L.Cpl. TOPPING, FITZGERALD to 4.5 F.A. for CONTAMINATION & Trench STANRRIDGE " " " FRICOURT aur MAXWELL to aust "dug" QRENCH to BECOURT aur OCONNOR, HARDY, WRIGLEY to return to S.h.9.P.	JMack
"	11/9/16		Note work of rotation arranged for. Fatigue party of 4 N.C.O. & 20 men actual for. Three party tips for unplesant cap, sit me & fixed. Infected BECOURT road more or less drawn up. Infected ADS labour large ircing & etc. s. " infected 9th Gud. aur.	JMack

T2134. Wt. W708—776. 500000. 4/15. Sir J. C. & S.

Army Form C. 2118.

WAR DIARY
or
INTELLIGENCE SUMMARY.
(Erase heading not required.)

Instructions regarding War Diaries and Intelligence Summaries are contained in F. S. Regs., Part II. and the Staff Manual respectively. Title pages will be prepared in manuscript.

Place	Date	Hour	Summary of Events and Information	Remarks and references to Appendices
ALBERT	18/8/16		As 4 sectn. Two sectns. Cotn. Pu "Coy" RESNYCH Billet - in rest for baths to RECOURT wood area.	ST
"	19/8/16		Church. FRICOURT Avenue. STAN RIDGE & theol. work. Head aspect. RECOURT. FRICOURT. CONTALMAISON. Transpd. Lines from & 7/8 Rev.D in reserve. Fatigue party of 30 men arrived at RECOURT. Genl. routine & refresher work.	ST
"	20/8/16		Routine work. RECOURT and cleared T.F.M. Lectures conducted	ST
"	21/8/16		RECOURT & CONTALMAISON with DADMS. New area allotted to 1st Section Red Scheme Corps troops during stay in III Corps area. Area Essex 17 through "CREST (exclusive) RECOURT wood, CONTALMAISON Letters funded (G. F—— party for " Royal Scots & Ro. Fuchw Class Instructr for A&D ligh.tn. Fatigue party Cheny. RECOURT wood. Infecte roads into all over area. Special infectn. FRICOURT PEAKE wood - SAUSAGE Valley. RECOURT. Scheme drawn up.	ST
"	22/8/16			ST

T2134. Wt. W708-776. 500000. 4/15. Stn J.C. & S.

WAR DIARY
INTELLIGENCE SUMMARY

Place	Date	Hour	Summary of Events and Information	Remarks and references to Appendices
N. of ALBERT	24/8	24/8/16	Moved Bn. to ALBERT & men had rest to enable rest of Bn. to cover up supplies etc. also the fact that it would be the be slightly shelled on three consecutive days. At request of Corps wanted 1. 20 d. further sanitary inspects & reports submitted. There are difficulties in cleared by latrines as men refuse to use present enemy trenches for these though some very clean, many shoe holes in latrines. Still the 4 dug affected the field over RECOURT line latrines (4) suggested to fill over RECOURT wood. There is absolutely nothing whatever of value to Except at the farm in savage valley Full dugout now available at RECOURT wood with Sergt BLENCH (Ept Epping. Kirk howells O'Connor & Pte Nodarly.	1775
"	24/8/16		Visited RECOURT & Savage Valley. Dismantled cable to Sergt BLENCH. The work in progress formerly	Aty

Army Form C. 2118.

WAR DIARY
or
INTELLIGENCE SUMMARY.
(Erase heading not required.)

Instructions regarding War Diaries and Intelligence Summaries are contained in F. S. Regs., Part II. and the Staff Manual respectively. Title pages will be prepared in manuscript.

Place	Date	Hour	Summary of Events and Information	Remarks and references to Appendices
W. of ALBERT E.8.B.2.	25/8/16		Recent wet + heavy of being placed by working party of 30. Am fills latrine pits. Placed in the wood. Shell well 06 ½ full which fills was dug.	
	26/8/16		Examined trench "SAUSAGE" valley. Shell infested decourt area. Note infection.	S.I.7.1
			Latrine area E of Albert now requires of 14 H.L.I. & gas cinder. 2 latrines badly placed. Sub. Latrin placed in trench thougt SAUSAGE valley. Lt. C. ALKINS & GRAHAM signed work. Note infection & cubicle ink used on Head infected got cracked supt infect.	S.I.7.I
	28/8/16.		Head sent to hand over. Went out to hand over. Walk recely with Ordpt of flying station 72 per week Pad BECOURT fatigue party. Waltin - Col. may bring chlorine supply with the week	A.F. 7/16
	29/8/16		Infect of contact ink freeway. Seal spot of little and S of ALBERT 7	S.I.7.

T2134. Wt. W708—776. 500000. 4/15. Sir J. C. & S.

WAR DIARY
or
INTELLIGENCE SUMMARY.
(Erase heading not required.)

Place	Date	Hour	Summary of Events and Information	Remarks and references to Appendices
	29/8/16		Units refitted & continue work. 2 C/M TOPPING special leave	APS
	29/8/16		Further new system of trying out all cook offs. Sgt CRANNIN replaced 2 C/M TOPPING with colored sgts	APS
E.26.8.2	3/9/16 6		Estab. & Infects. unch. as usual. Expires a complete rest & sound sleep. Good rest to Lee. BECOURT Wood. Supply of "c" rat to be sent to CONTALMAISON heavy shelling of SAUSAGE VALLEY. Inferno wk the wk. Glass has been smashed & the custody agent. She is a good deal of safe which is valuable sought. As troops late in to close but may elves have taken in quantity.	APS

Unit Inspection — Appendix 1.

Name of Unit

Cookhouses ① Situation, Surroundings
② Cleanliness, — cookers, Pots etc.
③ Protection of food from flies, dust etc
④ Cooks — washing facilities, overalls etc
⑤ Disposal of refuse, greasy water etc.

Water ① Source ② How Stored?
③ Is it treated? ④ Inspection of water cart

Flybreeding — How is manure dealt with?
  Incidence of flies

Billets, bivouacs, tents etc ① Cleanliness
② Ventilation, ③ Receptacles for refuse.
④ Protection from weather, dampness etc.

Personal ① Facilities for bathing,
ablution benches etc, disposal of washing
water ② Incidence of lice. Any powders
or greases used to prevent?
③ Is the general health of unit good?

Latrines ① Position ② Structure & type.
③ Are they well looked after?
Urine Pits — Ditto —
Disposal of camp refuse
Facilities for washing clothes.
Are disinfectants used freely for latrines, etc
Advice given, where error exists
Result . . . . .

WAR DIARY
or
INTELLIGENCE SUMMARY.

Army Form C. 2118.

14

140/1734

CONFIDENTIAL WAR DIARY

32 Sanitary Sec 15th Div

of

SEPTEMBER 1916

J.H.Hawkes Capt. RAMC (T)

O.C. San Sec. 32

COMMITTEE FOR THE
MEDICAL HISTORY OF THE WAR
Date 30 OCT 1916

WAR DIARY
or
INTELLIGENCE SUMMARY.
(Erase heading not required.)

Army Form C. 2118.

Place	Date	Hour	Summary of Events and Information	Remarks and references to Appendices
E 8 a 32 E 7 d 4.3 "Kemmel" Hut	1/9/16		Continued work along the trench etc. Laying roads for sanitary area. Inspection visits to look over work and examined routine inspection work.	
"	2/9/16		Spent in FRICOURT. CONTALMAISON. FRICOURT TRENCH. Not difficulty in allotting camps to fulfil certain sectors, indeed enough for our destruction work.	975 915
"	3/9/16		Spent out to BECOURT area. Interview with sanitary officers of 1st and 4th Canadian shields. Inspect in E8c.D. to E7 & 4.7. Supply of bren started at 20 Acres 7 square supply. Potable by O.O. train. We pumped supply tomorrow. Routine inspection work.	977
"	4/9/16		Getting new camps in order, work all roads etc. Defects show that there is a heavy wastage of supplies shelters (few corr. of shop to Library), fully counted for by large numbers of flies. The weather is now able of all & empty out the trails should channel.	978

WAR DIARY
or
INTELLIGENCE SUMMARY

Army Form C. 2118.

Place	Date	Hour	Summary of Events and Information	Remarks and references to Appendices
ALBERT SHEET E7b43	5/9/16		Route inspected & contracts let.	
			Spent unit received one billet spent to report	
	6/9/16		but will start to begin & receive one - not our sanitary area - No latrines provided & cooks in a little furthest of sleeping area. Pretty ring defeated & field mud	
	7/9/16		Spent went to receive one Cafes filled & Co were troops and filled the latrines & manure chutes. Visited Cafes to engine the horses with regard to flurry Corps; Stars & BASE out. Route inspection & contracting work.	
	8/9/16		Fülle latrines clay man route called as follows: Decent Road 2, Debout Hood, Hood 8, Decent Rd 6, CONTALMAISON, were SAUSAGE VALLEY 5, Decent trough 1. LOZENGE 6 (?) to CONTALMAISON 2, CONTALMAISON 2. Spent went to CONTALMAISON the tracks SAUSAGE valley etc. Great improvement in the area generally.	

WAR DIARY
or
INTELLIGENCE SUMMARY
(Erase heading not required.)

Army Form C. 2118.

Place	Date	Hour	Summary of Events and Information	Remarks and references to Appendices
ALBERT (about) E.7 & 4	8.9.16		The redress of drunken & boisterous troops offers itinerary...	
			hardly died to auto-holiday of food & current officers	
			messes not handle fastic case, all the returned post	
			(last few) battalion etc. & officers' messes is very bad.	J/7
				J/8
	9/9/16		Routine inspection and Construction work	J/9
	10/9/16	6	Section working except in enemy Construction work	
	11/9/16		Construction & inspection work at usual. BECOURT area	
			very crowded — at last 9 Battalions & 6 Coys of	
			Royal Latrine excavation, inefficient — reason than to	
			deal with the last of 24 inch boring (light & very	
			unsatisfactory state — referred to SS in 3rd Div. Should	
			be Every Labor at CONTALMAISON.	
			first affacts arr'g to excavation of trenches at air lay	J/10
			dealt with	
	14/9/16		Routine work. Road sections also fatigue pack	J/11
			inspection of BECOURT area	

Place	Date	Hour	Summary of Events and Information	Remarks and references to Appendices
E7 & 43	13/9/16		Analysis of all recent reports on the water establishment. Explicit in that of all water supplies where found and with details required. Report only that there are 6 type supplies (R.E.) and 2 fm. field service wells — all newly good quality water (Liverpool ones) Routine inspection & construction work	J.T.A
"	14/9/16		Arranged with staff Sergy. detail of work along with 20th dividn Reported to OC 47 F of a for duty with above Simmis Coy MARTINUICH R.O.C. wk 47 field ambulance at CONTALMAISON. Sect. work as usual. Jack G.S.O. party working round ALBERT.	J.T.A
	15/9/16		Lorry cleaney wounded	J.T.A
	16/9/16		Sectn work as usual. Reynd. sectn from Z.A	J.T.A
	17/9/16		Routine work. Nothing special to report	J.T.A
	18/9/16		Section resting	J.T.A

WAR DIARY
or
INTELLIGENCE SUMMARY

Army Form C. 2118.

Place	Date	Hour	Summary of Events and Information	Remarks and references to Appendices
E 76 4.3	19/9/16		23rd Div. took over 18th Div. area. In accordance with Corps arrangements Sanitary Section continued to supervise front line. Interview with ADMS re. 23, 30 divn. Sanitary Officers so as in every 6 weeks with regard to detail of work. Ref. to area etc.	
"	20/9/16		There are not RECOURT. CONTALMAISON. all ADMs 20 ch North work.	
"	21/9/16		Kept interview with DDMS III Corps re estimative etc.	
"	22/9/16		Motor cyclists placed at all posts, 2 motor cyclists & 1 contalmaison under instruction from L/Cpl FITZGERALD. Speaks out to PEAKE wood area — arrange for supply of latrines for use of 23 Div that area. Joint re inspection Contalmaison & note 2 Newfoundlands arrived. W. WALSH Schwaben D.A x-RAY bulged survoyn to refuse infection L/Cpl WRIGHT COLLINS evac to refuse infected L/Cpl MAXWELL wounded G.S.W. R/L wound Sound signed dearly shelled Pte RICHARDS. wds L/Ch wtth.	

Army Form C. 2118.

WAR DIARY
or
INTELLIGENCE SUMMARY.
(Erase heading not required.)

Place	Date	Hour	Summary of Events and Information	Remarks and references to Appendices
Erlys	22/9/16		Water tank & contents. Heard not recount seen.	S/H
	24/9/16		Section nothing except for necessary inspection & construction work. Found ago body odour see hunger list est-	J/H
	25/9/16		by exhibits. Turned aged received to HQ cap. In rest.	
			Special visit to contamination. Inspected return and water supply. Large number of flies but return to be installed. Got 3 little crocs. 20th supply carefully examined. Petrol tins sent up to MARTINPUICH for O.C. to see. Later to be taken by M.O. next for wells as at rest and returned for analysis.	J/H
	26/9/16			J/H
	27/9/16		Water inspection inc. contents of return etc. Heard out to CONTAMINATION "Jerome up" of victim at MARTINPUICH. Reviews complaints re caps mostly return	J/H
			our own	

WAR DIARY
or
INTELLIGENCE SUMMARY

(Erase heading not required.)

Army Form C. 2118.

Place	Date	Hour	Summary of Events and Information	Remarks and references to Appendices
E7 b 43	28/9/16		Examination of July cases of suck returned from MARTINPUICH - all other billets destroyed by shellfire. Pulled 3 cell 3 "no metals". Took specimen to AMIENS for further examen. Route work by motor.	
	29/9/16		Sanitary Conference at ADMS office. Interview with ADMS 23rd Div. Two cases Enteric fever. (I New "May" available)	
	30/9/16		Special inspection of CONTALMAISON to O.C. I was H.Q. of Anzacs. H.Q. at group. Steps taken re latrines etc. Note infected contacts work.	
			The system recently adopted of keeping sanitary returns is in our opinion very incomplete. Owing to many discoveries, reliefs of men O.C.'s etc. Our stage, it is difficult to get fatigue parties. That is to obtain natives, the period between in but is rect so difficult to maintain & report to infection.	

140/18/4

15th Div.

32nd Sanitary Section.

Oct. 1916

COMMITTEE FOR THE
MEDICAL HISTORY OF THE WAR
Date -9 DEC. 1916

WAR DIARY
or
INTELLIGENCE SUMMARY.

CONFIDENTIAL DIARY

SANITARY SECTION 32 Ptd 15 Div

OCTOBER 1916

J.H Hawkes (Cpl. RAMC)
O.C. San. Sec. 32

Army Form C. 2118.

WAR DIARY
or
INTELLIGENCE SUMMARY.
(Erase heading not required.)

Instructions regarding War Diaries and Intelligence Summaries are contained in F.S. Regs., Part II. and the Staff Manual respectively. Title pages will be prepared in manuscript.

Place	Date	Hour	Summary of Events and Information	Remarks and references to Appendices
ALBERT AREA E7C43	1/10/16		Advanced Squad moved to coping ground S° of SHELTER WOOD X27 B 64	APX
	2/10/16		Sent to DDMS III Corps re attack of coping ground. Found Adv. we should take over B Sect III Corps but that Sqdt move to Pick axe to X27 R 64. Visited ADMS 15th Div. Returned Sa Office re "Div who use hony B case Inst. were filled, when etc	APX
MONTIGNY III CORPS	3/10/16		Div. conf. Arng'd mode re rations etc	APX
			Visited ADMS 23 Div re Cmflest (Scott reduced)	APX
"B" SANITARY AREA	4/10/16		Forward Sqd moved to MONTIGNY. Conf with 46 L & C & EBRTS re re return re letter. Outlined work in case with Staff Sergt. Returned DDMS 3rd Corps who found me Act 10 Ch 3 in Cmfld to attend to section. Arng'd mode for clerg etc	APX
	5/10/16		Sect'n rating - Left workshp. Cmg'g Elect etc	APX

T2134. Wt. W708—776. 500000. 4/15. Sir J.C. & S.

Army Form C. 2118.

WAR DIARY
or
INTELLIGENCE SUMMARY.
(Erase heading not required.)

Instructions regarding War Diaries and Intelligence Summaries are contained in F. S. Regs., Part II. and the Staff Manual respectively. Title pages will be prepared in manuscript.

Place	Date	Hour	Summary of Events and Information	Remarks and references to Appendices
	6/10/16		Section Officer (Capt. Dawson) evacuated sick. Capt. Proud 46th Field Ambulance takes command. Inspection of area commenced.	ap
	7/10/16		Despatched men to work outlying portions of area as follows :- 3 to FRANVILLERS, 2 to LAVIEVILLE and 2 to BRESLE. Town Majors of above places visited and programme of work arranged.	ap
MONTIGNY III Corps "B" Sanitary Area.	8/10/16		Visited Town Majors of BETHENCOURT, FRECHENCOURT, MONTIGNY and ST. GRATIEN. Work to be done by Section discussed.	ap
	9/10/16		Forty three P.B. men for sanitary work in area arrive.	ap
	10/10/16		Surveyed MONTIGNY and ST. GRATIEN.	ap
	11/10/16		Surveyed BETHENCOURT and FRECHENCOURT.	ap
	11/10/16		Surveyed FRANVILLERS and LAHOUSSOYE also camps between FRANVILLERS and BRESLE	ap
	12/10/16		BRESLE and LAVIEVILLE also adjoining camps surveyed.	ap
	13/10/16		Camps between LAVIEVILLE and ALBERT surveyed.	ap

T2134. Wt. W708-776. 500000. 4/15. Sir J. C. & S.

WAR DIARY
or
INTELLIGENCE SUMMARY.
(Erase heading not required.)

Army Form C. 2118.

Place	Date	Hour	Summary of Events and Information	Remarks and references to Appendices
	15/10/16		Sanitary arrangements required throughout area tabulated and workshops organized to deal with same.	AP
	16/10/16		Routine inspection. Works carried on by P.B. men inspected.	AP
	16/10/16		Visited MONTIGNY, BETHENCOURT and FRECHENCOURT.	AP
	17/10/16		Visited ST. GRATIEN and district.	AP
	18/10/16		Town Major EAUVIEVILLE interviewed re works to be done there also M.O. re no duties of P.B. men. attd.	AP
	19/10/16		BRESLE and adjoining camps visited. Duties of sanitary section of P.B. men attached discussed with Town Major.	AP
	20/10/16		Visited FRANVILLERS and LA HOUSSOYE. Town Major interviewed.	AP
	21/10/16		Camps between FRANVILLERS and ALBERT visited. Town Major BRESLE also Mayor interviewed re removal of manure from yards. Manure dump site chosen.	AP
	22/10/16		Routine inspection. ST. GRATIEN visited and sites for two manure dumps fixed. Sgt. Bench put in charge of the work of removal of manure and other refuse from this district.	AP

Army Form C. 2118.

WAR DIARY
or
INTELLIGENCE SUMMARY.
(Erase heading not required.)

Instructions regarding War Diaries and Intelligence Summaries are contained in F. S. Regs., Part II. and the Staff Manual respectively. Title pages will be prepared in manuscript.

Place	Date	Hour	Summary of Events and Information	Remarks and references to Appendices
	23/10/16		P.B. men returned to 8/10/16 despatched to Town Majors as follows: — FRANVILLERS 2, LAHOUSSOYE 4, BETHENCOURT 10, BRESLE 10, ZAVIEVILLE 10. Large fatigue party at ST GRATIEN – removal of manure and other refuse commenced. Existing sanitary conveniences repaired. Nuisances henceforth dealt with.	SR
	24/10/16		BETHENCOURT, FRECHENCOURT and MONTIGNY visited. Destruction to sanitary conveniences by civilians enquired into.	SR
	25/10/16		Camps and district between LAVIEVILLE and ALBERT visited. Nuisances caused by troops halting here while on their way to and from the line are gradually being dealt with.	SR
	26/10/16		ST. GRATIEN visited – works referred to on 23/10/16 progressing. Several new sanitary conveniences have now been installed. Town Major of MONTIGNY interviewed re sanitary arrangements at Chateau & surroundings.	SR
	27/10/16		Visited FRANVILLERS and LAHOUSSOYE. Both places are now in good order. Destruction to sanitary conveniences by civilians enquired into.	SR
	28/10/16		LAVIEVILLE and BRESLE inspected. Very little manure as far	SR

T2134. Wt. W708—776. 500000. 4/15. Sir J. C. & S.

WAR DIARY
or
INTELLIGENCE SUMMARY.

(Erase heading not required.)

Army Form C. 2118.

Place	Date	Hour	Summary of Events and Information	Remarks and references to Appendices
	28/10/16		removed by civilians owing to scarcity of labour and transport otherwise toils places are in good order.	pr
	29/10/16		Routine work - nothing special to report.	pr
	30/10/16		Camps between ENIEVILLE and ALBERT inspected. Semi-permanent sanitary conveniences for troops passing through are being installed.	pr
	31/10/16		ST. GRATIEN - Artillery left yesterday - removal of manure not yet complete. Water-points visited. Work at ST. GRATIEN almost at a stand-still owing to movement of troops.	pr

Army Form C. 2118.

WAR DIARY
or
INTELLIGENCE SUMMARY.
(Erase heading not required)

140/1903

9/2/16

CONFIDENTIAL WAR DIARY

3z Sanitary Section 15th Div.

November 1916

COMMITTEE FOR THE
MEDICAL HISTORY OF THE WAR
Date 31 JAN. 1917

A. Jury
Capt Ramc(T)
OC Sanit Sect 32

Place	Date	Hour	Summary of Events and Information	Remarks and references to Appendices
	Nov 1916			

WAR DIARY
or
INTELLIGENCE SUMMARY.
(Erase heading not required.)

Army Form C. 2118.

Place	Date	Hour	Summary of Events and Information	Remarks and references to Appendices
MONTIGNY III Corps B Sanitary Area.	1/11/16		ST. GRATIEN visited - No Town Major meantime. Improvements proceeding slowly. Arrangements at Chateau MONTIGNY inspected. Improvements suggested.	AD7
	2/11/16		BEHENCOURT and FRECHENCOURT visited - Town Major interviewed re manure removal.	AD7
	3/11/16		Visited FRANVILLERS and LAHOUSSOYE. Nothing special to report.	AD7
	4/11/16		Visited BRESLE and LAVIEVILLE. Question of ablution benches discussed. Remainder: sawing timber etc from Engineers Dump.	AD7
	5/11/16		Part of Section resting.	AD7
	6/11/16		Attended special meeting of sanitary officers at III Corps A.B.	AD7
	7/11/16		Section handed over to Capt. Shury who takes command from this date.	
	8/11/16		Inspected MONTIGNY and BEHENCOURT, found satisfactory. Latrine not satisfactory, constructors work proceeding. Visited FRECHENCOURT but did not complete inspection.	AD7
	9/11/16		Visited Field Cashier Amiens. Interviewed ADMS. Interviews visitors Section N.C.O. Investigated case of poisoning at FRANVILLERS.	AD7
	10/11/16		Visited FRECHENCOURT and with MO 1st Div Schol inspected village. Urgent need of improvement here especially in regard to incinerators & manure removal.	AD7

WAR DIARY
or
INTELLIGENCE SUMMARY.
(Erase heading not required.)

Army Form C. 2118.

Place	Date	Hour	Summary of Events and Information	Remarks and references to Appendices
	10/9/16		Further visit FRECHENCOURT, inspected Rest Camp and interviewed O.C. 5⁰ Irish Horse & arranged of Same. Visited T. Mgr BEHENCOURT & discussed employment of P.B. men	A.S.I.
	11/9/16		Inspected ST. GRATIEN. Conditions supremely bad, mainly owing to want of latrine. Interviewed 2. Major who promised to take steps to improve condition. Interviewed Sub'in inspector held fag parade	A.S.I. A.S.I.
	12/9/16		Routine inspection & orderly room details	A.S.I.
	13/9/16		With D.D.M.S visited ST. GRATIEN, FRECHENCOURT and BEHENCOURT. Arranged sanitary arrangements new School at MONTIGNY; starts construction of Bailleul C/o incinerator at FRECHENCOURT	A.S.I.
	14/9/16		Reported D.D.M.S Corps & discussed condition of area. Took steps for forming permanent P.B. sanitary squads for villages. Visited FRECHENCOURT & BEHENCOURT, at latter place noted commencement of disinfecting routine at old LAUNDRY	A.S.I.
	15/9/16		Visited FRECHENCOURT interviewed M.O. & O.C. R.W.Y & arrival of manure. Improved Corps incinerator & dead met refuse left by S. Irish Horse.	A.S.I.
	16/9/16		Visited FRECHENCOURT, inspected S. GRATIEN, some improvement here, no place adequate for Baths, but portable shower could be installed. Inspected MONTIGNY	A.S.I.

Army Form C. 2118

WAR DIARY
or
INTELLIGENCE SUMMARY
(Erase heading not required.)

Instructions regarding War Diaries and Intelligence Summaries are contained in F. S. Regs., Part II. and the Staff Manual respectively. Title Pages will be prepared in manuscript.

Place	Date	Hour	Summary of Events and Information	Remarks and references to Appendices
	17/11/16		Inspected FRANVILLERS; fair canteen here, but civilian manure a great problem. Investigated cases diphtheria (?) at Behencourt.	A.S.J.
	18/11/16		Routine inspection; orderly room detail.	A.S.J.
	19/11/16		Special visit to D.A.D.M.S. 15 Corps re order to transfer 4 men to S.O. ALBERT. This is a great misfortune & likely to disorganise Section.	A.S.J.
	20/11/16		Orderly room; routine inspection; sent squad to ALBERT.	A.S.J.
	21/11/16		Visited FRECHENCOURT, with M.O. inspected. School billets. Inspected completed school arrangements MONTIGNY.	A.S.J.
	22/11/16		Routine inspection; investigated case of diphtheria (?) at FRECHENCOURT.	A.S.J.
	23/11/16		Inspected LAVIEVILLE and BRESLE. Interviewed the respective T. Mayors. Both villages fairly satisfactory except in regard to paths to sanitary areas & civilian manure. Pond at LAVIEVILLE needs treatment or pumping out. Special visit BEHENCOURT & Bellen 23 & Horse Lines. Drew attention generally to the question.	A.S.J.
	24/11/16		Special visit Abbevé. Discussed matters relating to Sector & administration of area. Understood that we are shortly to take over L. Forward area. Routine inspection.	A.S.J.
	25/11/16		Routine inspection; orderly room detail.	A.S.J.

Army Form C. 2118.

WAR DIARY
or
INTELLIGENCE SUMMARY.
(Erase heading not required.)

Place	Date	Hour	Summary of Events and Information	Remarks and references to Appendices
	26/11/16		Attended Conference forms' Office. Routine inspections	
	27/11/16		Special visit A.D.M.S. S.O.L Found worked out & discussed matters relating to itineraries & section	
	28/11/16		Visited S.O.L Found area & discussed further details of removal. Special visit A.D.M.S.	
	29/11/16		Visited A.D.M.S. Removal to L Found area completed & A.D.M.S. notified.	
	30/11/16		Personnel cleaning & settling into new quarters. Conference of Section N.C.Os; inspection areas decided upon and allotted. New Corps are among very large unit requiring number of fatigue men.	

Army Form C. 2118.

140/903

WAR DIARY

INTELLIGENCE SUMMARY.
(Erase heading not required.)

CONFIDENTIAL WAR DIARY Vol 17

Month of DECEMBER
1916

Capt A E Jury. RAMC (T)
O.C. 32 Sanitary Section. 15th Dv.
L. Forward Area
III Corps
IV Army

A E Jury Capt
O.c. 32 Sanitary Section

COMMITTEE FOR THE
MEDICAL HISTORY OF THE WAR
Date 31 JAN. 1917

Place: Dec 1916

WAR DIARY
or
INTELLIGENCE SUMMARY.

Army Form C. 2118.

Place	Date	Hour	Summary of Events and Information	Remarks and references to Appendices
FIELD	1/12/16		Routine inspection. Special visit CONTALMAISON and district	A59
	2/12/16		Routine inspection. Special visit CHESHIRE LABOUR BAT? SAUSAGE VALLEY and CORPS REST STATION BECOURT.	A59
	3/12/16		VISIT ALBERT, routine inspection	A59
	4/12/16		Routine inspection. Visited Town Major, BECOURT CAMP. Fun parade	A59
	5/12/16		Routine inspection; Special visit BECOURT WOOD Open & BATHING STATION	A59
	6/12/16		Routine inspection; Special visit CONTALMAISON, visited OC S.MIDLAND F.A. Inspected Laundry A & B sub SANITARY AREAS	A59
	7/12/16		Routine inspection; Special investigation ventilation of NISSEN HUTS. Visited CHESHIRE LABOUR BAT?	A59
	8/12/16		Very wet, but some inspection work carried on	A59
	9/12/16		Very wet but some inspection work carried on	A59
	10/12/16		Very wet. Routine inspection; Special visit A/ADMS 47 Division enquiring into incidence of Diarrhoea	A59
	11/12/16		Routine inspection. Special visit MARTINPUICH WATER POINT. Day wet	A59
	12/12/16		Very wet. Routine inspection, Special work POZIERS DISTRICT.	A59

Army Form C. 2118.

WAR DIARY
or
INTELLIGENCE SUMMARY.
(Erase heading not required.)

Instructions regarding War Diaries and Intelligence Summaries are contained in F. S. Regs., Part II. and the Staff Manual respectively. Title pages will be prepared in manuscript.

Place	Date	Hour	Summary of Events and Information	Remarks and references to Appendices
Field	13/7/16		Routine inspection. Special visit to La Boiselle District	
	14/7/16		Routine inspection. Visited ADsMS at ALBERT. Visited MOLINS-AUX-BOIS.	
			Lectured VI Dw.l School on SANITATION.	
	15/7/16		Routine inspection. Special visit CONTALMAISON DISTRICT	
	16/7/16		Routine inspection. Survey visit SAUSAGE VALLEY, POZIERS ROAD LA BOISELLE & AVOCA VALLEY.	
	17/7/16		Routine inspection. Special visit N. and S. SCOTCH REDOUBT and N. and S. SHELTER WOOD. Visited ADMS	
	18/7/16		Routine inspection. Visited ADMS	
	19/7/16		Routine inspection. Visited SHELTER WOOD & SCOTCH REDOUBT Camps and ADMS	
			Inspected LA BOISELLE & POZIERS RD work	
	20/7/16		Routine inspection. Pay parade, 5 reinforcements arrived.	
	21/7/16		Routine inspection. Visited S's ALBERT. Special visit ALBERT-BECOURT RD. Very wet	
	22/7/16		Routine inspection. Visited CONTALMAISON. Visited DADMS. Very wet.	
	23/7/16		Routine inspection. Special pay parade. High wind.	

Army Form C. 2118.

WAR DIARY
or
INTELLIGENCE SUMMARY.
(Erase heading not required.)

Instructions regarding War Diaries and Intelligence Summaries are contained in F. S. Regs., Part II. and the Staff Manual respectively. Title pages will be prepared in manuscript.

Place	Date	Hour	Summary of Events and Information	Remarks and references to Appendices
	24/10/16		Routine inspection. Visited Camps 1 & 2. Interviewed Area Inspectors	89
	25/10/16		Visited SHELTER WOOD Camp & RUM TRENCH Highwood	89
	26/10/16		Routine inspections. Visited Arms. Visited SHELTER WOOD & SCOTCH REDOUBT Camps - very unsatisfactory - reported them to A/DMS. 33 men from Brigades attached this day	89
	27/10/16		Routine inspections. Visited SHELTER WOOD (N & S) & BRIGADE Camps. Special visit BECOURT WOOD & LA BOISSELLE Redoubts very wet	89
	28/10/16		Routine inspections. Visited A/DMS & "2" a Camps. Visited MOLIN'S AUX BOIS POSNT. Lecture XV Brit School - SANITATION -	89
	29/10/16		Routine inspection. Visited A/DMS. Special visit SHELTER WOOD and SCOTCH REDOUBT Camps also ACID DROP Camp - some improvement	89
	30/10/16		Routine inspections. Visited A/DMS. Special visit SHELTER WOOD & SCOTCH REDOUBT Camps. Improvement maintained. Visited CONTALMAISON.	89
	31/10/16		Visited SHELTER WOOD & SCOTCH REDOUBT Camps. Work well in hand. Telnet decompleted network. Visited SAUSAGE VALLEY	89

14.6/1941

15th Div.

32nd Sanitary Section.

Jan. 1917

COMMITTEE FOR THE
MEDICAL HISTORY OF THE WAR
Date 4.–APR.1917

Army Form C. 2118.

WAR DIARY
or
INTELLIGENCE SUMMARY.
(Erase heading not required.)

Vol 1 8

Confidential Diary

Sanitary Section 32 att. XI Div

JANUARY 1917

A.S. Jury Capt RAMC(T)
OC 32 Sanitary Section

Army Form C. 2118.

WAR DIARY
of
INTELLIGENCE SUMMARY.
(Erase heading not required.)

Instructions regarding War Diaries and Intelligence Summaries are contained in F. S. Regs., Part II. and the Staff Manual respectively. Title pages will be prepared in manuscript.

Place	Date	Hour	Summary of Events and Information	Remarks and references to Appendices
	1/1/17		Routine inspection. Visited Shelter Wood (N+S) & Scotch Redoubt (N+S) Camps & discussed details of drainage & rat pits with Pioneer Officer. Visited CHAPES SPUR & SAUSAGE VALLEY also La BOISELLE district.	A/J
	2/1/17		Routine inspection. Visited ADMS - SHELTER WOOD & SCOTCH REDOUBT CAMPS - CONTAYMAISON BECOURT WOOD, AVOCA VALLEY - CHESHIRE RGT & RAILWAY ENGINEERS. Noted early appearance of flies in fair numbers.	A/J
	3/1/17		Routine inspection. Visited ADMS & informed him that flies seen in regard to flies discussed question of footbaths for huts. Visited SHELTER WOOD & SCOTCH REDOUBT Camp also BECOURT WOOD & CHAPES SPUR.	A/J
	4/1/17		Routine inspection. Visited ADM. Visited SHELTER WOOD - SCOTCH REDOUBT CAMPS. also PIONEER Camp, SAUSAGE VALLEY	A/J
	5/1/17		Routine inspection. Visited SHELTER WOOD & SCOTCH REDOUBT Camps also POZIERS RIDGE. Applied for initial supply of 'C' solution.	A/J
	6/1/17		Routine inspection. Morning & afternoon lecture & demonstration to sanitary squads 4 units. Visited SCOTCH REDOUBT & BRIGADE Camp.	A/J

Army Form C. 2118.

WAR DIARY
INTELLIGENCE SUMMARY.
(Erase heading not required.)

Place	Date	Hour	Summary of Events and Information	Remarks and references to Appendices
	7/1/17		Routine inspections. Morning & afternoon lectures & demonstrations to Sanitary Squads & units. Visited 92nd. SHELTER WOOD & BRIGADE Camps - met officer in charge's Pioneers & settled details. O.C. 50th Divl. Sanitary Section called.	OX
	8/1/17		Routine inspections. Visited 92nd. Submitted report to Adms & 2. Visited ACID DROP & PIONEER Camps & selected sites for latrine, ablution benches etc. GORDON Camp. Sent Vermorel Spray solution to 47th F.A. for transmission to Front Line.	OX
	9/1/17		Routine inspections. Visited 92nd. Visited with R.E. officer SHELTER WOOD S. to look out for new foot baths. SCOTCH REDOUBT (N. & S.) & CONTALMAISON. M.O. 9 Gordons called re disinfection. Referred to S.O. ALBERT.	OX
	10/1/17		Routine inspections. Visited 92nd. Afternoon morning lecture & demonstration to 2nd Batch 92nd Sanitary Squads. With '2' visited SHELTER WOOD (S) & SCOTCH REDOUBT (N. & S.) re latrine to foot bath huts. Pioneer officer informed me that Pioneer had been taken off the trenching spade work in those camps & that Infantry men armed be used for the purpose. Further visited the Camps in the afternoon visited progress of greenwork in SHELTER WOOD - South.	OX

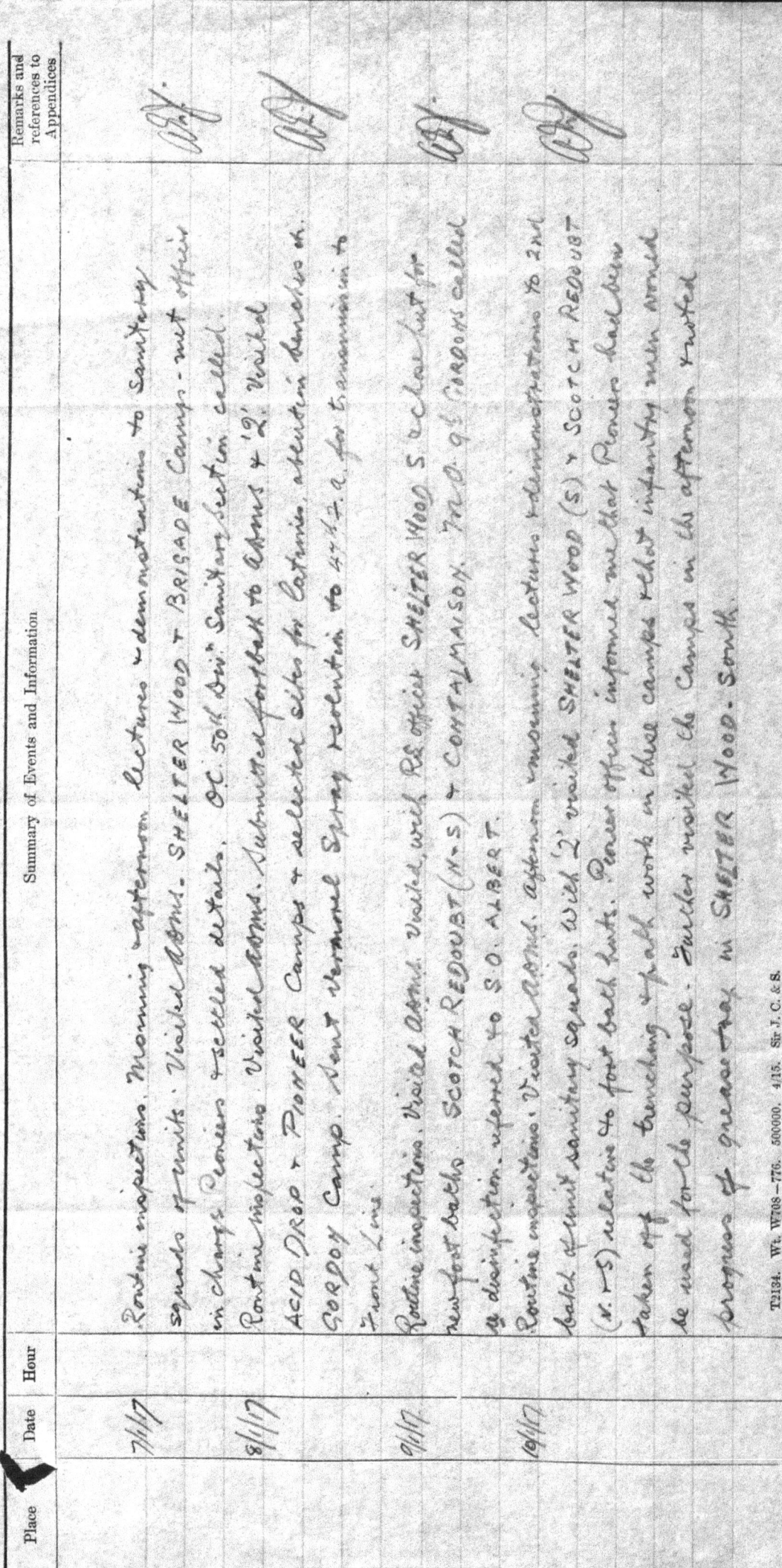

Army Form C. 2118.

WAR DIARY
INTELLIGENCE SUMMARY.
(Erase heading not required.)

Instructions regarding War Diaries and Intelligence Summaries are contained in F. S. Regs., Part II. and the Staff Manual respectively. Title pages will be prepared in manuscript.

Place	Date	Hour	Summary of Events and Information	Remarks and references to Appendices
	11/1/17		Routine inspections. Visited A.D.M.S. Lecture & Demonstration to 2nd Batch spent Sanitary Squads. Visited SHELTER WOOD South noted that great tar nearly complete. Instruction given to proceed with similar trap at SCOTCH REDOUBT (N) at once. Visited MOINS-AU BOIS & delivered lecture to school.	A.H.
	12/1/17		Routine inspections. Visited A.D.M.S. – CHAPES SPUR – SAUSAGE VALLEY. LA BOISSELLE – POZIERS. SHELTER WOOD (S) Bath benches & grease traps completed. SCOTS REDOUBT (S) Bath benches completed & grease trap well on hand.	A.H.
	13/1/17		Routine inspections. Visited A.D.M.S. – SHELTER WOOD (N + S) ACID DROP PIONEER VILLA – GORDON CAMPS. Ran Lorries this day.	A.H.
	14/1/17		Routine inspections. Visited A.D.M.S. – CONTALMAISON. ACID DROP PIONEER. SHELTER WOOD (N + S). SCOTS REDOUBT (N + S) Camp. LA BOISSELLE.	A.H.
	15/1/17		Routine inspections. Visited A.D.M.S. 4th Div. San. Officer. Visited SHELTER WOOD (N + S) SCOTS REDOUBT (N + S) L/Cpl. STANBRIDGE wounded this duration of hand, on the incinerator at SCOTS REDOUBT (S) – after treatment resumed his duty. Output by return that SHELTER WOOD (N) Camp will be struck this week.	A.H.

T2134. Wt. W708-776. 500000. 4/15. Sir J. C. & S.

WAR DIARY
INTELLIGENCE SUMMARY.

Army Form C. 2118.

Place	Date	Hour	Summary of Events and Information	Remarks and references to Appendices
	16/1/17		Routine inspection. Visited A.D.M.S. Visited SCOTS REDOUBT (N.+S.) SHELTER WOOD (H.+S.) Camps. CONTALMAISON + units in AVOCA VALLEY + LA BOISELLE area. Heavy fall of snow on night of 16/17 - 1.17	A.9.
	17/1/17		Owing to snow fall, spent majority of section at H.Q. Visited A.D.M.S. SHELTER WOOD (S) - a shed destroyed new attention shed blown last night. SHELTER WOOD (S) - Ohio Camp in process of being altered. SCOTS REDOUBT (N+S), CONTALMAISON WATER POINT. Two O.Rs. admitted to reinforce Section	B.9.
	18/1/17		Routine inspection work carried out, but owing to snowfall construction work curtailed. Visited A.D.M.S. + SHELTER WOOD Camps.	A.9.
	19/1/17		Routine inspection. Visited A.D.M.S. Visited SHELTER WOOD. SCOTS REDOUBT + VILLA Camps.	A.9.
	20/1/17		Routine inspection. Visited A.D.M.S. Visited BRIGADE + SHELTER WOOD Camps and units in BECOURT + CHAPES SPUR district. Packs &c. arrived in improvement.	A.9.
	21/1/17		Routine inspection. Visited A.D.M.S. Visited forward area, SAUSAGE VALLEY + LA BOISELLE	C.9.
	22/1/17		Routine inspection. Visited H.Q. SCOTS REDOUBT Camps, CONTALMAISON, CHAPES SPUR BRIGADE TRANSPORT LINES, AVOCA VALLEY + POZIERS ROAD.	C.9.
	23/1/17		Routine inspection. Visited A.D.M.S. ORDERLY ROOM details not of May	D.9.

Army Form C. 2118.

WAR DIARY

INTELLIGENCE SUMMARY.
(Erase heading not required.)

Instructions regarding War Diaries and Intelligence Summaries are contained in F. S. Regs., Part II. and the Staff Manual respectively. Title pages will be prepared in manuscript.

Place	Date	Hour	Summary of Events and Information	Remarks and references to Appendices
	24/1/17		Routine inspection. Visited Bomb. Visited AKESTER WOOD (N+S) SCOTS REDOUBT (N+S) POZEER, ACID DROP & GORDON CAMPS. SAUSAGE VALLEY. AVOCA VALLEY. LA BOISELLE.	
	25/1/17		Routine inspection. Visited A.D.M.S. VISITED MOULIN AU BOIS. Lectured XV Div. School.	
	26/1/17		Routine inspection. Commenced construction bath for new area. Reinforcements arrived.	
	27/1/17		Routine inspection. Visited A.D.M.S. Units of 2nd Australian Div. Sanitary Section to take day in place of "take over". Withdrew advance party this day.	
	28/1/17		Orderly Room. Pay Parade.	
	29/1/17		Visited A.D.M.S. + "Z" in charge for carrying of equipment to "G" Survey for me. Lorry promised for tomorrow but question of whom to attend now for a day or so.	
	30/1/17		Visited A.D.M.S. Arranged final details of move to bath area.	
	31/1/17		Visited A.D.M.S. Proceeded to WARLOY with Section attached men leaving small hand cart to Australian Sanitary Section.	

140/1991

15th Div

32nd Sanitary Section

COMMITTEE FOR THE
MEDICAL HISTORY OF THE WAR
Date 4 APR 1917

Feb 1917

Army Form C. 2118.

WAR DIARY
or
INTELLIGENCE SUMMARY.
(Erase heading not required.)

Vol 19

Confidential Diary

Sanitary Section 32 att XV Div

FEBRUARY 1917

A.E. Yuryk (?)
Captain (?)
O.C. 32 Sanitary Section

WAR DIARY
INTELLIGENCE SUMMARY.
(Erase heading not required.)

Army Form C. 2118.

Place	Date	Hour	Summary of Events and Information	Remarks and references to Appendices
	1/7/17		Section and attached men assembling into new groups. Interviewed Town Major & gender ready. Have been allocated.	A89
	2/7/17		Visited VANDENCOURT and CONTAY. Read later posts in reported from BECOURT	A89
	3/7/17		Visited HQ at BAZIEUX, also visited BRESLE, FRANVILLERS & LAVIEVILLE	A89
	4/7/17		Visited HQ ANZAC. Pioneer fatigue parties to Town Major & HQ ZANE	A89
	5/7/17		Visited Divrni. Inspected BAZIEUX, FRANVILLERS & LAVIEVILLE and found ANZAC Sanitary Section opening there. Trained in this house & latest instructions	A89
	6/7/17		Visited BAZIEUX, CONTAY & VANDENCOURT. Arrangements been made. VANDENCOURT & CONTAY has to working matenance & improvements, however put there places into a satisfactory sanitary condition & maintain same pending arrival of ANZAC Section.	A89
	7/7/17		Visited G.A. and was informed that except for opening Sour assistance of ANZAC Sanitary Officer, the section could rest until further orders. Workers to be informed no should carry out movements as departing troops. Sanitary inspection. WARLOY & CONTAY Visited MOLINS-AU-BOIS & environments. Divisional School.	A89
	8/7/17			A89
	9/7/17		Leave granted. Landed me to Capt. Proud & Fab. & Ambulance. Report. Cancelled stayed night in ANIE 95	A89

Army Form C. 2118.

WAR DIARY
INTELLIGENCE SUMMARY.
(Erase heading not required.)

Instructions regarding War Diaries and Intelligence Summaries are contained in F. S. Regs., Part II. and the Staff Manual respectively. Title pages will be prepared in manuscript.

Place	Date	Hour	Summary of Events and Information	Remarks and references to Appendices
	10/9/17		Returned WARLOY. Reported O.S.G.M.S. Jork my Section from Capt. Proud	O.S/
	11/9/17		Reported S.A.S.M.S. Instructions that Section were to meet an attached to 47th L. Amb. Visited CONTAY + BAZIEUX. Returned attached men to their units.	O.S/
	12/9/17		Preparing for move. Overhauled stores & equipment. Lost Lorry to 47th F. Amb.	O.S/
	13/9/17		Inspected WARLOY, CONTAY, BAZIEUX + VANDENCOURT.	O.S/
	14/9/17		Moved Section to BEAUVAL + billeted there.	O.S/
	15/9/17		Moved Section to BRETEL + billeted there.	O.S/
	16/9/17		Moved Section to FORTEL + billeted there.	O.S/
	17/9/17		Moved Section to HERICOURT + billeted there.	O.S/
	18/9/17		Moved Section to NEUVILLE-AU-CORNET + billeted there	O.S/
	19/9/17		Moved Section to DUISANS + billeted there. Reported to O.C. and Town Major S.A.S.M.S. etc. Gave S.M. no information as to ever probably - arranged to commence arrest in work in anticipation.	O.S/
	20/9/17		Saw S.A.S.M.S. but had no further instructions for Section. Reserve "2" + arranged to be retained by H.2.	O.S/

Army Form C. 2118.

WAR DIARY
or
INTELLIGENCE SUMMARY.
(Erase heading not required.)

Place	Date	Hour	Summary of Events and Information	Remarks and references to Appendices
	21/2/17		Reported D.D.M.S. no instructions to hand. Saw Town Major re undertook to take C/a in charge of the street cleaning & incineration squads. Posted Sgt Inchley temporarily to Town Major AMBRINES	OBJ
	22/2/17		Survey of DUISANS commenced. Visited AGNES-LES-DUISANS & inspected Baths there. These are working at full personnel & cannot accommodate 7th Division. Found likely spot for erection of Baths at DUISANS	OBJ
	23/2/17		Detailed entire of Section turned on numerance. Reported to D.D.M.S. necessity for Baths. Sent lorries to SAVY for timber but owing to congestion of sanctioning officer it returned empty.	OBJ
	24/2/17		Reported D.D.M.S. and him visited 2" & Baths. Pointed out in connection with lines of 2' to approach Baths. Agreed to 2' fort 2" lines to be attached to Section for sanitary fatigues. Visited Baths at AGNES-LES-DUISANS	OBJ
	25/2/17		Reported D.D.M.S. Visited hutted Camp at E. and trolleys-sanitary arrangements inadequate, with 12' & CRS, visited with Divisional Sanitary Coll to draw up Sano retainments.	OBJ
	26/2/17		Attached men reported own first Coal Generators - no nails available. Visited HABARCQ. Town Major out. Took over R.E. stores from Sanitare, who	OBJ

A8634 Wt. W4973/M687. 750,000. 8/16 D.D. & L. Ltd. Forms/C.2118/13.

WAR DIARY
or
INTELLIGENCE SUMMARY

Army Form C. 2118.

Place	Date	Hour	Summary of Events and Information	Remarks and references to Appendices
	26/7/17	Cont	stated that his section was examining the village notwithstanding fact that majority of troops therein were XV Div.	(A)
	27/7/17		Investigated case of Marado at AMBRINES reported absent them. Visited LOUEZ found own troops magnificent Condition there. No IV Div troops in village. Reported freely in writing to OC 6th & 12th Bns. Sgt Called Dec discovered quarters of HABARCQ. Decided that when not be made in the village burned received the N.C.O. & notify me in order that NCOs in absolute supervision being to avoid if/Law restrictions being small to draw material. This empedite dates in constantial book. Cpl TOWNEND proceeded to England to join Cadet Unit. Detailed for H.Q. duty in his stead L/Cpl DUYSTAY.	(A)
	28/7/17		Routine inspection. Special visit to Prisoner Burny DUISAYS which is not well under control. Visited Hutch camp – interviewed men Labour Batt permitted at rest in new lattrine pits upon arrangement. Feeding for material owing to lorry being unable to take rest.	(A)

B. Spun/Ram C.T.
Capt Sanitary
OC 31 Sanitary
IV Section
Div

www.ingramcontent.com/pod-product-compliance
Lightning Source LLC
Chambersburg PA
CBHW081359160426
43193CB00013B/2064